Women and War Jenny Matthews

Jenny Matthews

'There is perhaps no woman ... who could look down upon a battlefield
covered with slain but the thought would rise in her, "So many mothers'
sons! So many months of weariness and pain while bones and muscles
were shaped within; so many hours of anguish and struggle so that
breath might be!" No woman who is a woman says of a human body,
"It is nothing!"'

Olive Schreiner

Pluto Press, London
in association with ActionAid

Jenny Matthews is a documentary photographer working with Network Photographers. Since 1982 she has been working on a world wide project looking at women and war.

She studied at the University of Sussex and then worked for the British Council in Brazil. In the 1970s she taught in a comprehensive school in London and then at an Urban Studies Centre, before becoming a photographer.

Since 1982 she has worked as a photographer, documenting social issues in Britain and abroad. She has worked extensively in Latin America, the Middle East, Africa and Asia for all the major development organisations. Her photographs have been published in magazines and newspapers around the world.

In 1986-7 she produced a large exhibition on Women in Central America which opened at the Impressions Gallery in York and toured to London, Newcastle, Liverpool, Bristol and Plymouth. In 1998 her exhibition 'Women and Conflict' was at the Royal Armouries, Leeds as part of Photo 98, and was then shown in London, Milan and Perpignan.

First published in the United Kingdom by
Pluto Press
345 Archway Road, London, N6 5AA

www.plutobooks.com

ISBN 0 7453 2073 2

© 2003 Jenny Matthews, London

Original publisher
Mets & Schilt uitgevers, Amsterdam (2003)

Book design
Victor Levie & Barbara Herrmann, Amsterdam

Lithography & printing
Arcari SRL Industria Grafica, Mogliano Veneto

British Library Cataloguing in Publication Data
A catalogue record for this book is available from
the British Library

act!onaid

ActionAid is an international development organisation that works with poor and marginalised people in the developing world to eradicate poverty and overcome the injustice and inequity that cause it. We work with nine million people in 35 countries in Africa, Asia, Latin America and the Caribbean.

Our peace and reconciliation work in countries like Burundi, Sierra Leone and Ghana has ranged from re-establishing social relationships, trust and open dialogue between neighbours to high-level mediation and international lobbying.

www.actionaid.org

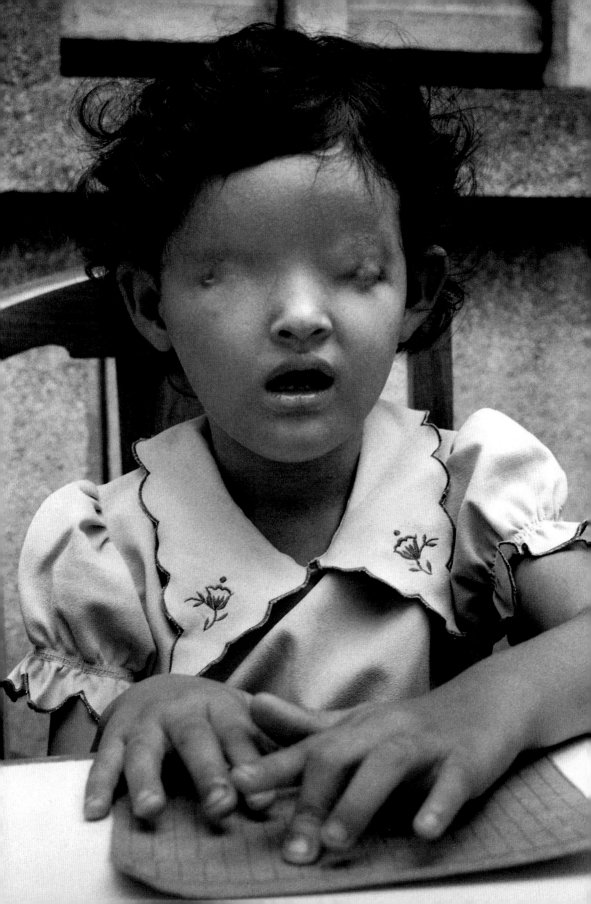

Introduction

The little girl was carefully tracing the dots, learning to read. I was focussing my camera on her fingers but my mind was focussed on where her eyes should have been. Phuong was born without eyes, her mother presumed to have been poisoned by Agent Orange, the chemical dumped on forests during the Vietnam War by American planes, to strip off the vegetation and deny cover to the Vietcong. Although when I photographed her in 1990 the war had long been over, the chemical had seeped into the ecosystem to wreak havoc on the next generation. Wars might end, but the consequences linger on – in Vietnam's case a large number of miscarriages and deformed babies.

The picture of Phuong, an eight-year-old with no eyes, was hard to take – it was one of those moments when a sense of outrage at the repercussions of war on the totally innocent makes clicking a shutter seem like a futile gesture, although she is also one of the reasons why I started taking pictures – to poke away at the world and record the way some things are, but shouldn't be. Vietnam was the country that shaped my politics in the sixties, this was the first war I protested against and which made me aware of the part film and photography play in recording history. Every time I print Phuong's picture and study the space where her eyes should be I try to imagine a life without sight or any awareness of light and colour.

My darkroom is full of spirits. There is Consolée, mutilated in Rwanda, who, left with only a few fingers, has great difficulty doing even the simplest tasks. There is Razia in Afghanistan. When I photographed her in 1996 she was working for a western aid agency, proud of being a female chowdikar. Then she lost her job and was virtually confined to her home for five years – the Taliban regime that forbade the patter of heeled shoes, the red flash of nail varnish, even singing, was not going to tolerate a woman stoking the office boiler, but it was wonderful to re-photograph her in 2001, tentatively putting on make-up for the first time in ten years.

There are joyous moments frozen in the dark too – war brings out the best as well as the worst. In Bosnia and in Haiti I met women who were somehow eking out the last bit of lipstick, getting their hair done, determined to look as good as possible in spite of the rubbish life was throwing at them.

As bearers of life, women usually have a much more emotional relationship to conflict – as mothers, wives, lovers they are the ones traditionally left behind with someone to lose, but war and peace do not divide neatly on gender lines. Although women are more often innocent victims and peace groups from Northern Ireland to Israel to Serbia tend to be dominated by women, they can kill too, and viciously, as seen in the genocide in Rwanda.

From the beginning I was interested in covering foreign stories – starting with Central America in the early eighties, a bit off the map for the British media but an exciting place with revolutionary groups fighting guerrilla wars in the mountains. Nicaragua had just had a revolution, the new Sandinista government was young and energetic and trying to put its idealism into practice. That seemed a good place to visit and Christian Aid gave me a commission to document the lives of women. The commission was enough to pay half a plane fare, but with a minimal lifestyle and some plastic money it worked out. I have been doing variations on that commission ever since.

One visit led to another and I learnt about war. The ugly side of American politics, post Vietnam, where training 14-year-olds to fight in El Salvador, destabilising the economy of Nicaragua and devastating the ethnic community of Guatemala, were on the agenda. Although I have often worked where the pictures in the news were of the frontline confrontation, I was more interested in what was going on behind the scenes, and that usually involved looking at how women were holding everything together. Some of the wars that I've tiptoed around have been major international conflicts – the Balkans, Middle East, Rwanda, Afghanistan – but others have been practically invisible. At the end of 2002 when the world was focussed on Iraq, I went to the east of Uganda and was horrified to find people's lives decimated by fighting over cows – the fallout from other wars in the region has meant cheap automatic weapons are available, and cattle rustling has become big business, with the tyrannised victims herded into camps and easy prey to the HIV virus.

I haven't been everywhere and this is not a complete record of world conflict, but my take on recent history, recognising the lives of remarkable women, ordinary people surviving as best they can. As I've travelled I've kept diaries and the notes from these accompany the photos. All my work has been done in co-operation with a whole network of people – journalists, friends, fixers, drivers, translators, development workers. Without them it would be hard to even leave home. It has been a great privilege for me to be a photographer, to wander into other people's lives, often uninvited but usually made embarrassingly welcome. I have lurked round some nasty corners of the world and come across the raw edges of life and death – an infinity of sorrow and fear but more often than not tempered with the hope that things will be better for the next generation.

Thanks

Massive thanks to my fantastic friends who've been there when I've come home, who have made suggestions and decisions and made sure I had a social life. Special thanks to Louis and Theo for being wonderful boys and making me part of their lives. Peter Kennard has been a constant source of inspiration and encouragement.

On the practical front, thanks to: Chris Boot, for introducing me to the very pleasant world of Dutch publishing. Jan, Maarten and Pleun at Mets & Schilt have been a delight to work with, and Anne Beech at Pluto has been a great editor and support. Thanks to Ian Denning for designing a brilliant first dummy and to Victor Levie and Barbara Herrmann for making this book and to Neil Burgess for starting the ball rolling. Gary Wilson and Stuart Keegan have been careful and committed printers. The staff and photographers, past and present, at Format and Network have been a wonderful source of support as have my overseas agents, Grazia Neri in Milan, Marion Schut-Koelemij in Amsterdam, Elka Kroll and Magda Rudzka in Warsaw.

Each trip has involved a whole network of people making it all possible – especially drivers and translators, thanks to them all. Each photograph has taken me into someone's life – above all I am greatly indebted to everyone I photographed – thanks to all those who started as strangers, for their generosity of spirit, their infinite kindness and their faith in what I was doing.

To organisations that have supported me: At ActionAid – Lyndall Stein and Laurence Watts; at Africa Rights – Rakiya Omar; at Care International, Chloe Bayram; at Christian Aid – Joseph Cabon; at Oxfam – Geoff Sayer; at Save the Children – Alan Thomas; at Sightsavers – Neil Thorns, and Geoff Ryan at the Salvation Army who made an impossible trip possible.

To travelling companions: Lindsey Hilsum – for her succinct knowledge of the world and a friendship that began in a horrible camp in Zaire, Fiona Macintosh, for amazing times in Nicaragua, Ros Young, who gave me a home, help and more in Gaza; Holly Aylet, Christine Aziz, Simon Norfolk and Harriet Logan for adventures in Afghanistan and Iraq; Kevin Toolis for sharing a desperate time in South Sudan; Esther Mujawayo for Rwanda; Nicola Peckett in Nepal, Cathy Scott-Clark and Adrian Levy for excitement in Burma, Glenys Kinnock for introducing me to Eritrea and South Africa, Jenny Rossiter for Angola and Olwyn and Chris Mason for Ethiopia.

Parveen The mother

An hour's drive from Baghdad, we come to a dissident Iranian army base, hidden away in the midst of a dry scrub landscape. Here 5,000 soldiers are earnestly training to attack Iran. Around one third of them are women and 70% of the commanders are female. Many of the women soldiers are mothers, some left children in Iran, others have sent them into exile – they used to live at the base before the Gulf War made it too dangerous. Parveen Firozan is a tank driver. She has left her one-year-old son in Teheran.

'I was a prisoner for nine and a half years, sent there when I was still in high school for selling (opposition) newspapers and supporting the mujahadeen. I was in prison in 1988 and witnessed the massacre of political prisoners. When people were executed in prison the trial would only last a minute – they would read your name and the verdict – either more prison or death. They would write the time of the execution on the wall. Sometimes we saw ropes hanging from the gallows and knew there had been executions the night before. We heard the crying relatives on Thursday nights at the mass graves. I survived because of love for what I believed in. My conviction that what I was doing was right. In prison with me there was a mother of four who was arrested because she was wearing nail varnish. She was put in a dark room and her hands were put into a sack of cockroaches.

I was released in 1990 but I felt I was in a bigger prison. I had a terrible life in Iran because I was always in conflict – I couldn't go back to an ordinary life because I had seen some of my best friends killed by the regime – all my memories were with them – I'd shared every excitement with them and they were all dead. I was looking for a way of getting rid of this split personality so after my release I thought it would make things more bearable to marry someone like me.

When I was 33 I had a child – a boy called Sebehr. His paternal grandmother had had four of her children executed so I couldn't leave him with her. He was one year old. I thought of women in prison – how they had to give birth there – but somehow those children survived, so I decided that I could leave him. For the first two months I always dreamt of him. I was always worried about him getting hurt or being treated badly by the grandmother I left him with – but I had to come to terms with leaving him. I mustn't allow myself to limit my feelings to one child – mine. We have to fight to get rid of this regime.

The night before leaving I didn't sleep at all – I thought how was he going to be brought up without a mother. I collected all the photos of him – looking at them is like a film. I took him to his grandmother's. I didn't tell her I was leaving. We said we were going to a party but I left the house key and documents with her. I could feel the child knew something was up. When I see a film and there's a baby in it takes my mind back – the same if I see an advert for baby milk. I haven't heard from the grandmother so I don't know how my son is. I remember when mothers were released from prison their children wouldn't recognise them.

Here I'm a gunner on a tank – in the past that was unimaginable – when I first saw a tank I thought how can this monster move? I was frightened when the guns were fired near me. At first it was difficult to lift tank shells. The noise in the turret, the smoke – it was all very alien and difficult, but eventually the tank became like putty in my hands and it got so my heart started to throb when I heard the tank engine.'

Iraq, February 9th 1999

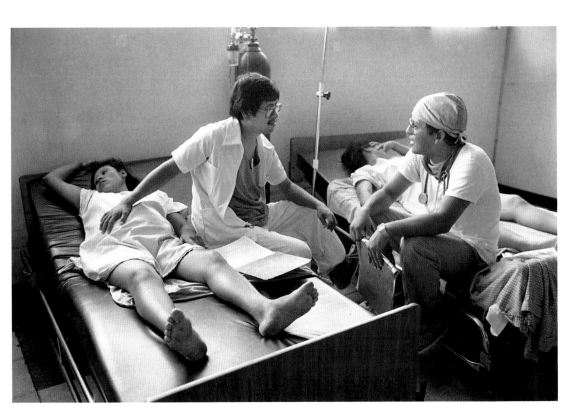

Managua, Nicaragua, November 25th 1985

Frustrating exchange of phone calls trying to get permission to work in the maternity hospital … eventually get hold of director and latin expansiveness kicks in – no problem, come straight away. Urged into the 'expulsion' room to witness birth of a baby – totally miraculous, so fantastic to see life beginning. In the labour room a couple of doctors sit chatting about baseball whilst the women in labour are in a completely different world.

> Panajachel, Guatemala, April 20th 1984

Early morning, in brilliant bright light, people make patterned strips outside their homes, vibrant mosaics in bright colours, done with flower petals or paper. This is for the Good Friday procession to walk on as it parades around the town visiting the altars that have been set up to represent the stations of the cross. After morning service indigenous women appear with candles and lead the statues of Jesus followed by the Virgin Mary around the streets. It seems very appropriate that women are carrying Mary since she is the hard act that Catholic women have to follow – the ideal mother, the pure wife, the heavy cultural burden.

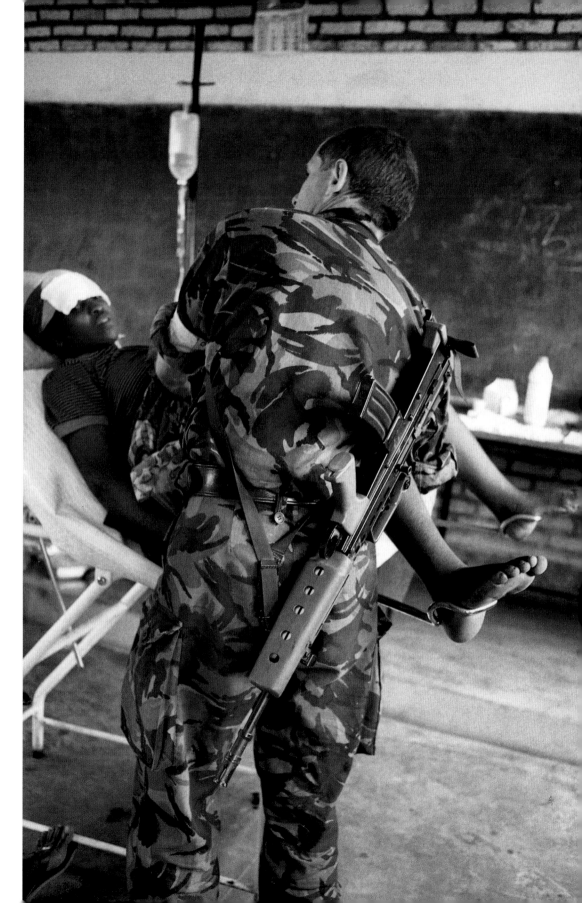

<< La Sopresa coffee farm, Matagalpa, Nicaragua, November 27th 1984

State of alert, rifles being handed out, tanks on the streets of Managua – everyone prepared for a contra attack from Honduras. With the agricultural union, travel four hours in a jeep to the mountains of Matagalpa (I dutifully clutch the grenade I've been given, very thankful there's no need to use it).

We go through drizzle soaked hills to a coffee plantation that has just been burnt out in a contra attack with 14 people killed. Fifty Miskito families were moved here four years ago from the dangerous Rio Coco area, now they are homeless again. Told that a pregnant woman was killed nearby and the baby cut out of her – a surviving pregnant woman seems terrorised and bewildered, standing in the smouldering ruins of her home besides the destroyed processing plant.

< Kibeho Refugee Camp, Rwanda, August 29th 1994

The British Army have replaced the French in what's known as the Turquoise zone (area of camps now housing Hutus who fled their villages after the genocide but didn't get as far as Zaire). They have set up a clinic in the teeming Kibeho camp, a two-hour drive from their base. Find Major Palmer, a British army psychiatrist, with a pregnant woman who has miscarried one of the twins she was carrying. Comment on the bizareness of doing a gynae examination with a machine gun on your back – told those are the orders. Situation tense. No one knows how it's going to pan out.

Near Freetown, Sierra Leone, October 22nd 1999

On the edge of town, a ramshackle house is home for around 20 pregnant girls and new mothers aged 14 to 18; most were abducted by rebels and taken by them to be sexual partners when the city was attacked in January 1999. Their room is immaculately tidy – each has a sleeping mat and a small plastic bag of clothes and toiletries. The babies are well cared for but, when we talk about plans for the future, most would like to have their children adopted, to be able to start anew without this reminder of their past.

Their housemother tells of a couple of girls throwing stones at dogs – she asked them about it, thinking they were frightened and might have been hurt by dogs. 'No,' they said. 'We want to see blood.'

> Freetown, Sierra Leone, October 13th 1999

With ActionAid team, visit projects working with single mothers – most have lost husbands, many were abducted and returned from the bush pregnant. Need to make sure children grow up loved and cared for – so they don't become the violent child soldiers of the future. For this the young women need some sort of financial security. It's hard to get a job in a town teeming with unemployed youth hanging out on street corners. Hairdressing is one skill always in demand and in a shack in the middle of the busy waterfront market young mothers learn how to make the complex arrangements of extensions and plaits, producing fantastic sculptures.

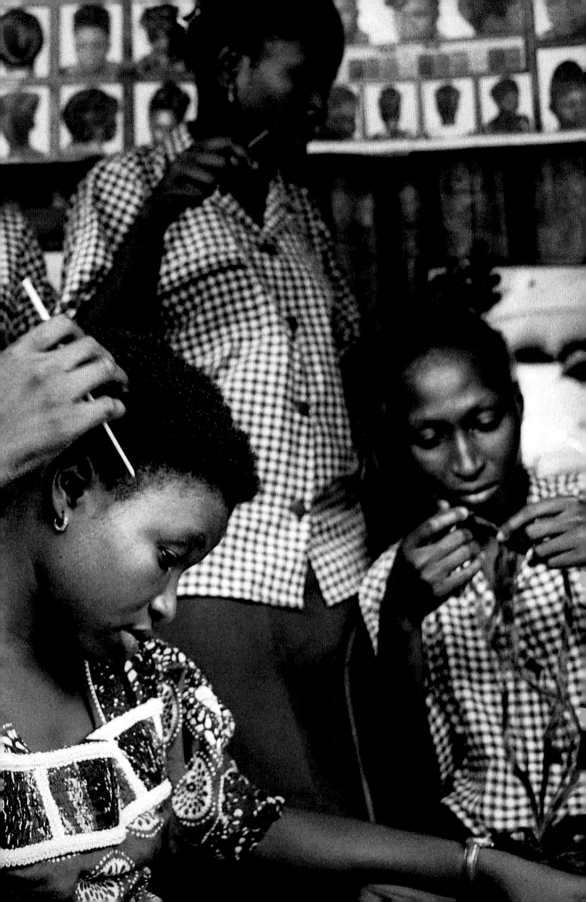

Magoro Camp, Uganda, December 12th 2002

Over one third of the new mothers in the camp are under 16. Some are married – in Eastern Uganda daughters are a valuable commodity, worth seven cows in normal times. Parents have a particular urgency to marry off daughters as soon as possible so that, with the bride price they receive, they can then marry off sons before the animals are stolen. Other girls get pregnant because they are hungry and the promise of a small present – some food, a petticoat or a pair of panties, is enough for them to consent to sex.

> Congo/Rwanda border, November 18th 1996

Up at 6 a.m. and walk up to the border where the refugees are camping before crossing back into Rwanda – everyone is exhausted having spent a couple of days on the run after Kabila ordered them to leave. They are very apprehensive of crossing back into the country they fled after the genocide, committed by their 'side'. Early morning activity in full swing – people wrapped in blankets huddle around smoky fires, everyone asks for biscuits, lots of medical cases waiting for attention. Peer into an empty tent and see a little bundle wrapped in a lace tablecloth secured with sellotape – overwhelmed by the painful thought of a woman giving birth by the side of the road, the baby dying and then having to leave the body behind.

Ajiep Camp, South Sudan, August 1st 1998

18-year-old Ayak Agau at the burial of her daughter.

A sad morning. In the drizzle, watching the burial of
those who died in the night, shaving the head, closing
the eyes, laying to rest. Those for whom aid was too
late – the handful of corn, transported at great expense
failed to save two-year-old Adut. Ayak's child is the
victim of hunger, but she knows nothing of the
Sudanese war's hidden agenda, where hunger is
manipulated and exploited. While the mother weeps,
the baby's aunt and grandmother break off her ankle
bracelets and place the body in a foetal shaped hole.

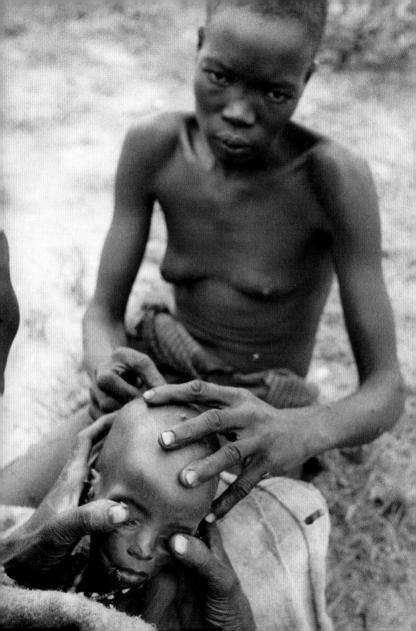

> Messica, Mozambique, November 12th 1986

In spite of being in the midst of a country at war, hear just one bit of artillery fire in the night. No transport, not a lot of food, families surviving on next to nothing, but lots of warmth, talk of politics, resilience. In the cool of the evening meet a soldier walking carrying his baby son, savouring time with him before he returns to the front in the morning.

>> Ajiep, Sudan, August 1st 1998

In spite of the atmosphere of death and despair, life goes on. A new mother suckles her baby.

>>> Shan State, Burma, November 25th 2000

Nung Hfu, 32, mother of three including a baby who was born in the camp.

In the midst of the bamboo jungle nestles a camp for displaced people. It looks quite idyllic – a neat row of palm thatched houses – but once we start talking everyone has stories of being harassed by the Burmese army, of forcible relocations, men shot for not being able to carry the army's goods, and villagers killed when they tried to return to collect rice from their fields. Half of the children in the tiny school are orphans, and they all tell painful stories of seeing their parents killed. These villagers are being protected by the Shan State Army, which means they are now at war with Burma, destined to eke out a precarious existence under constant attack.

>>>> Kabul, Afghanistan, December 8th 2001

Doctor Hamida continued to work under the Taliban, both at her job as a surgeon in the hospital and at her clinic. 'In the Taliban time it was good for us women doctors because we were some of the very few women who could work – even though we didn't get paid very often. For the last six months I've had nothing – I should get $30 a month. For us it's good for men and women to be separate, we are Muslims and in our culture that's how things are. In the clinic I'm seeing a lot of cases of nervous problems – a whole month of US bombing, with bombs landing all around us, affected many people, especially women worried about their families.'

Anoud Living with violence

Wednesday afternoon, Anoud Salim is having a facial. Normally she'd be at work, but in Gaza these days there's no such thing as normal. Over the last 18 months the narrow strip of land, home to around one million Palestinians, has been bombed, refugee camps raided and placed under curfew, and very few people can get out – that is travel more than 20 miles outside the strip. If you live in the southern camps, as half the population does, you can't go outside your camp. As a result many businesses, unable to get raw materials, have closed down. Anoud is on half time and half pay.

'My job is frozen. I can only work 15 days a month now, so on my days off I go to the beach, I go to restaurants, I treat myself. If you're not good to yourself, you're on the edge of death. You might as well give up on life. I keep phoning my friends in the West Bank to see how they're doing. One of them lives in the same building as a Hamas leader so it keeps being raided. Her husband was taken out with the others and had to stand in the rain for four hours. I want to pack in the good things before the Israeli army comes to Gaza. This week I got in my car and decided to drive around town. There are only three main streets in Gaza so it doesn't take long. I thought I might not be able to go out for three weeks. I decided you have to make the most of life, to live it to the maximum, you don't know what is going to happen next. We've got into the habit of living life spontaneously – sometimes this isn't good. When I drove around it was like a farewell to Gaza. My mother though, just stays inside. We are really fed up.

I dream one day I will wake up and there will be peace. I used to be a jeans and T shirt girl but now I'm dressing more smartly. I'm thinking I might die, I might as well use my clothes. You have to live in dignity. I'm only 22 and feel life should be waiting for me. Sometimes I feel why was I born in Gaza? If I was somewhere else I'd be having fun. I studied in Bir Zeit, a good university in Ramallah. After college I had 12 days of peace and then this second Intifada began. Most of my friends are abroad now. When I phone them I feel jealous that they are out having a good time but at least my life has more value. I know I belong here. Hanging out, meeting boys, drinking aren't the most important things in life. I think I need to find a goal. I look at my inner self then I laugh and think, what are you doing worrying about your inner self, get real. Cope with the present.

Tuesday was Holocaust Day and on Israeli TV they had a film about the Holocaust. I thought it was a nightmare. Everything that happened to Jews in 1942 is happening to us in 2002. The difference is the year. The film was about glorifying life – it was the story of Anne Frank. I felt she was just like me except she kept saying I hate Germans, and I don't hate Jews. After the programme I wrote a letter to the survivors asking them to support us because they know how to value life. We share the same fear, the same love of life. I wrote, "you know about suffering and surviving, you worked hard at building a country, you can't blame us for fighting for our rights. There's a value in life, let's not waste it."

Now there's not a lot to gossip about, it's not like the old times. Now it's always politics we talk about. Some of my friends have got engaged – planning a wedding can be a way of escaping what's happening around you.'

Gaza, April 9th 2002

Bogota, Colombia, May Day 1990

Overwhelmed to find that in a country of so much fear, with gratuitous violence always a possibility, thousands of people come out onto the street to celebrate May Day. A mix of trade unions, political parties, circus performers, lottery sellers, and a very vocal group of women protesting loudly against domestic violence. A pity that tear gas brings it all to an end.

> Suchitoto, El Salvador, May 7th 1986

Drive back from Suchitoto, avoiding the spent mortar cases that litter the road. At a blown bridge stop for a road check and ask to take photos – as it's 'Day of the Soldier' (as opposed to Day of the Secretary – Salvadoreans honour certain occupations with special days), the young lads strutting their stuff all seem to be in a good mood and unusually amenable.

>> Bogota, Colombia, May 1st 1990

Wandered around town – nervous because of so many exhortations to be careful, so many tales of violence, although chic shops and the usual array of downtown banks and smart restaurants make it feel like any city anywhere. An enormous cinema poster for Dolph Lungren as the Punisher, wielding a machine gun, adds to a feeling of insecurity.

<< Road to Bo, Sierra Leone, October 8th 1999

On the road back to Bo, just as it's getting dark, come to a road-block, guarded by the skull of rebel leader Hawai – the soldiers say he makes them strong. Peaceful here now but the atmosphere is redolent of fear and nastiness.

Road-blocks are where people with the wrong papers, no papers or maybe even the wrong expression are shot, where power games are played. In Zaire a crazed soldier with a grenade in his hand screamed at the car I was in until enough money was handed over to pacify him. In the North of Uganda, a boy in a woman's wig and a very big gun had my jeepful of adults bowing and scraping until we were waved through. In Chechnya there are so many road-blocks, some even within sight of each other, that just going to what passes as a market becomes a whole day excursion. Then the hassle of queuing and having papers checked is nothing to the fear, the beating heart, the dread of being taken away.

< Mostar, Bosnia, December 10th 1994

Driving back from Tuzla to get a plane at Split, stop in Mostar, or rather what's left of it. Amidst the ruins people are trying to get on with life.

> Gisenyi, Rwanda border, July 20th 1994

Walk down to the border, counting bodies on the way, 15 neatly wrapped parcels of rush matting, victims of cholera. Close to the control post itself the remains of those killed in the rush to cross the border at the weekend. And on to the most chilling site, a pile of arms taken off the fleeing killers as they crossed into Zaire – guns from the Hutu soldiers, but also a mass of machetes, knives, pounders, and assorted agricultural implements used by ordinary villagers to kill their ordinary neighbours.

>> Bisesero, Rwanda, May 14th 1996

A long rocky road up a steep hill. After we leave the village behind, the area is deserted. No children's laughter, no cooking smoke. Come across two men wobbling their way home, the worse the wear for banana wine. They take us to a field where the bones have been gathered together. Having heard the car, gradually people appear, a group of survivors, all men. They were under siege here. Most of the men and all the women of the village were killed, a couple hundred of the 800,000 victims of the genocide.

<< Grozny, Chechnya, June 7th 2000

Drive from Nasran to Grozny, only about 50 kms but with ten Russian checkpoints to go through it takes several hours. Some check papers, some search the vehicle. My cameras have become part of my body, carefully hidden. Sneak out to take a photo of the shot-up 'welcome to Grozny' sign. And then we come to the city of rubble – streets of chaos, ruined buildings on top of ruined buildings. At first there's no sign of life. Between Russian patrols, I sneakily take some photos – then a few women emerge.

Taus Belashanova, 36 years old, neatly scarfed, optimistically carrying a shopping bag, says she's come out to look for food. She starts crying when she talks about her 21-year-old son who she won't let out. She's terrified that the Russians will take him off to a filtration camp – the fate of most young men. Tales of death and torture in these camps. ... She wipes away her tears with her stumps: she lost her hands in a rocket attack during the first Chechen war. 'Tell them to stop shooting. The soldiers come and loot what's left of our homes, if we protest they threaten us with bullets.'

<< Grozny, Chechnya, June 7th 2000

Koka stands outside the remains of her home and cries for her daughter killed in Chatoy. She has a few rooms left amidst the rubble. 'People live here', has been painted on the wall.

< Grozny, Chechnya, June 7th 2000

Rosa Tournhudjieva, a widow like most women here, walking with one of her six children, voices the anger and despair of those left behind. 'It's all because of oil. The school has been destroyed, now there is nowhere for children to go. On television it says help has been given to Chechnya, but where is it? In nine months I've received 4 kilos of flour. It used to take 20 minutes to walk into the city but now with the road-blocks we have to go a longer way round and it takes two hours.'

> Shan State, Burma, December 2nd 2000

4 a.m. Shaken awake in soggy banana grove where have been trying to sleep off extreme fatigue wrapped in leaves. Told the Burmese soldiers know we are there and are coming after us. Five minutes later we're running across a stubble field and up a mountain. One hundred Shan soldiers move silently and invisibly, we trail behind, trying to get dressed as we stumble along. As the darkness seeps into daylight realise we are rushing through poppy fields – the confirmation we wanted that the Burmese are still getting villagers to grow opium. Desperately shoot a few frames, glad of the excuse to stop for a few extra seconds before continuing the torture of running up and down hills and along narrow ridges, careful to keep to the path because of the possibility of landmines off track. After several hours are told the threat has been dealt with and we slow down to chat with villagers and the cooks make the best lunch ever – rice and flowers.

< Guatemala City, September 4th 1985

Arrive in city, find hotel and go out for a stroll.
Bump into a full-scale riot with shop windows broken,
people looting and riot police and tear gas everywhere.
Team up with 'Aqui el Mundo' TV crew and spend the
next few hours cruising with them, taking photos of
people affected by the gas. Totally unprepared – am
very grateful for vinegar soaked hanky someone gives
me. Sight of army going by wearing gas masks and
machine guns at the ready is chilling.

Bamiyan, Afghanistan, 1997

New Year's Eve. High in the Hindu Kush mountains the
sun was shining on a snowbound town, home of the
giant Buddhas (blown up in 2001). People were shuffling
to and from market. Out of the bluest of skies a buzzing
became a silver plane. Bombs dropped. Life was
suddenly on the edge. The giggling group on their way
to market were now crowded into a snowy ditch with
me. Hearts beating faster. The Taliban were attacking.

> Kabul, Afghanistan, December 9th 2001

Murals were painted to teach people how to recognise
and avoid the various landmines which litter the
country. Now unexploded cluster bombs from the US
bombing have added to the potentially lethal weapons
lying around, traps for children looking for playthings.
In late 2001 food was dropped in bright yellow plastic
bags. The cluster bombs also had a bright yellow
plastic part.

Amoding Displaced from home

Amoding Keletesia has spent the last ten years living in a camp, one of several where almost 90,000 live after being terrorised by cattle rustlers. As we talk she passes the green leaves she has gathered through her hands to make sure they are dry and can be stored so that she'll have something to feed her family during the dry season when no other wild food will be available. I was told she had been raped by the Karamojong (the neighbouring tribe who have been stealing cattle with increasing violence) but was apprehensive about broaching the subject. She, however, came straight to the point.

'I don't mind talking about what happened to me because everyone knows about it and even my children saw it happening. There's nothing I can do about it – I was lucky to have some counselling and advice.

It was around midnight. Three men came and forced the door open. I was in one hut with my husband and the baby I was breastfeeding. The other children, seven of them, were in their hut. They made us all go outside, took my clothes off, and forced them to watch, my husband on one side, the children on the other, while they raped me one after the other. I was between life and death. They had guns and used them to beat my husband and three eldest children, one boy and two girls. While they were raping me, they were pressing one of the guns to my chest really hard.

These men were rebels of the area – this was in 1987 – who wanted to overthrow the government. We fled to the trading centre, but the next morning they came there and said why are you still around, go back to the village. I went to the nearest medical centre to get some injections, then we went back home but there was nothing there – they had taken the little money I had and all the household things. My husband was a veterinary assistant – they took his motorbike, all my gomasis (the long dresses with puff sleeves that Ugandan women traditionally wear) and all my cooking things. The only clothing I had left was a blouse of my daughter's – I wrapped this round my breasts and bottom and went to church to pray – it was only praying and believing in God that has given me the strength to carry on. We had to put grass on the floor to sleep on because they had taken the mattresses.

I still feel the pain where I was hit by the gun. Now we are here in this camp because of the Karamojong – it's been here for the last ten years and we come when we fear attacks. Even today we got a message that they are coming. That's why all the cattle have been put together and are here with us. Our village is only a couple of kilometres away but we prefer it here because it is guarded by soldiers.

When I was raped I was breastfeeding my last born. At first, for more than a year, my husband left me alone, he was watching my stomach, seeing if anything was going to happen there, whether I would be pregnant, but it didn't. Now we are old and have separate beds anyway.

When I was young, life was OK, I've grown old and haven't really felt myself since that incident. I still think about it – after that experience I've always been frightened when I see men with guns.

Life in the camp is not comfortable – some of the girls are forced to have sex. Everyone is very close together and many people drink. I go to the village to dig – we have sorghum, groundnuts, millet – not a lot, just enough to feed the family. This year the harvest was very poor, there might not even be enough seeds for next year, especially groundnuts.

My dream is for my children to finish their education and get jobs. I never went to school and can't read or write. My parents wanted the girls to marry, they didn't prioritise education for them.'

Ocorimongin Camp, Katakwi, Uganda, December 11th 2002

> **Tashiling Tibetan Refugee Camp, Pokara, Nepal, November 24th 2002**
Walking through Pokara involves running the gauntlet of Tibetan women, hunting in pairs, with small backpacks full of curios – mostly jewellery – chanting 'I give you good price, looking is free.' Times are hard. They have few customers as there are hardly any tourists because of the war between the government and Maoists.
The older Tibetans, stranded in Nepal since they arrived over 50 years ago when the Chinese invaded Tibet, are still waiting to go home.

San Salvador, El Salvador, August 17th 1983

Flying from Nicaragua to Guatemala I have a five-hour wait for a connection in El Salvador (vicious civil war well underway). Have the name and address of a priest working with displaced people. A long nervous taxi ride takes me to an imposing church. Find the priest, and am enthusiastically welcomed. Out the back are 800 people camping in a courtyard. Am totally overwhelmed.

In the midst of a tangle of people cooking, washing and playing, was a wonderful moment – and picture – some older women learning to read and write for the first time, thoroughly engrossed and finding deep pleasure in the midst of their uprooting. A roll of film later rush back to the airport and away.

> Tucson, Arizona, USA, August 13th 1985

Pre-breakfast swim in the pool. A phone call sets the house into a panic. A family of nine Guatemalans, including four children, have been picked up and detained by the Immigration department.

Winnie (my hostess) is part of the Sanctuary Movement, a solidarity network that looks after illegal immigrants from Central America. She rushes off to deal with the crisis. Angela arrives to do the cleaning – she's an 'illegal', from Guatemala. Her family paid £500 to a coyote (guide) to bring them across the border from Mexico when her brother was killed. She has five children but had to leave four behind – she doesn't complain about the sadness in her life. Cleaning is easier than her previous job in a trouser factory.

I take photos as she cleans the fridge, feeling disloyal to Winnie – the migrant domestic worker underneath the middle-class artist's poster rejecting housework.

< Mexico City, Mexico, August 26th 1985

To Neza, sprawling poor part of the city, and the romantically mis-named Pasaro Azul (Bluebird) – a squalid home for 24 Guatemalan refugees. 68-year-old Juana pines for home. 'Here is like a prison. I don't go out because I get lost and I don't like the smell of gasoline. I can't speak Spanish very well. I never went to school but I sent my son so things would be better. We had a terrible time finding enough money for his education – and then he was killed. Here I can't wear my traje (traditional clothes), I have to wear trousers, this is very difficult.'

Mexico City, Mexico, August 26th 1985

Candelaria and her children, refugees from Guatemala, wait for papers to go to the States. The assassination of Manuel's uncle terrified the family and forced them to flee, but this doesn't stop Manuel playing with his favourite toy, a gun.

< Calle Real Displaced Camp, El Salvador, October 14th 1985

Not an ideal day for a visit as a group are about to set off for a protest outside the cathedral – a few older people are left, including a TB patient patiently waiting for life to get better. 'We are here because of the repression of the armed forces. We couldn't stand it any longer. If you have a home they burn it, if you have a pig they kill it, if you have a pair of trousers they burn them.'

La Basilica refuge for displaced, San Salvador, El Salvador, October 1st 1985

A hairy motorbike ride across town clinging to the driver priest. We pull up to an elegant church. A fleet of Mercedes from a middle-class funeral is pulling away. We go round the back and into a smoke-filled hall. 700 people now live in what was once a basketball court. Most have not been outside for a couple of years – they come from FMLN controlled zones and would be very likely arrested if they left the security of the church. Babies and stacked bedding are everywhere. Mass is celebrated amidst women breast-feeding

and children playing in the sole tiny patch of sunlight. In one corner of the hall the tortilla team has been at work all morning. The lives of Central American women are dominated by the tyranny of the tortilla, a flat maize bread that is the region's basic food. It's eaten with beans if possible, but more often than not, just with salt. Women rise at 3 or 4 a.m. to begin the laborious task of making them. Maize is soaked with lime, drained and ground to a paste. The women pat this dough into rounds which are cooked on an open fire. A large family may get through 60 in one meal. At least refuges have encouraged women to cook together and share domestic labour.

< Deheisha Refugee Camp near Bethlehem, West Bank, April 26th 1988

A high wire fence surrounds the camp, the Israelis say it's there to stop stone-throwing. I go in through a turnstile, which makes it impossible for people to move quickly. The psychological effect is of entering a cage, of being controlled. All the small roads in the camp are blocked off with barrels and razor wire. When I return, years later, the turnstile is no longer in use, but the Palestinians want to preserve it as a monument to their experience as refugees.

Goma, Zaire, July 19th 1994

'The problem has moved up the road', said the UN spokesman, referring to the million plus people who crossed the border at the weekend, the guilty and their communities fleeing the genocide in Rwanda.

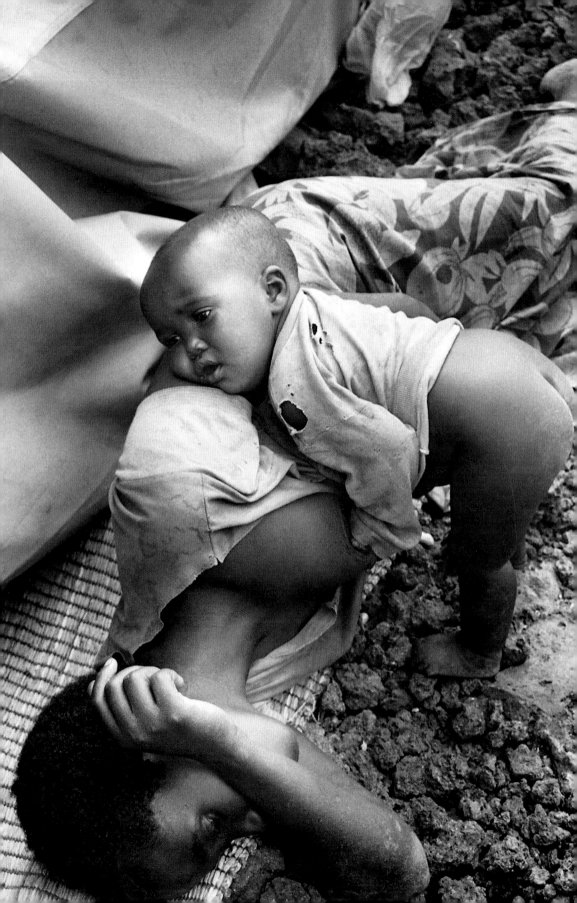

Munigi Camp, Goma, Zaire, July 21st 1994

'The horror, the horror'... This is the Heart of Darkness.
Already 300 suspected cases of cholera – across town
dead bodies wrapped in rush mats, tied at the neck
and ankles, left by the side of the road. I start off
counting them but after 50 give up. A short ride out of
town there's meant to be a refugee camp, Munigi, but
it's no more than a floor of hard black lava strewn with
sick people. There's no water, no comfort.

> Congo/Rwanda border, November 18th 1996

Largish groups of people are still crossing the border
(Kabila's new government of Congo has decided the
refugees from Rwanda have to return home). Most are
returning with fewer possessions than they arrived
with two years ago.

>> Kibeho Camp, Rwanda, March 17th 1995

Two hours drive from Gikongoro, a camp for 280,000
displaced clings to the hillsides. They prefer the
insecurity of camp life to returning home to their
villages and the wrath of neighbours they betrayed.
On the surface the camp looks innocent enough, but
this is also home to the perpetrators of the genocide.

> Zagreb station, Croatia, December 2nd 1991

Although Zagreb is the capital of a country at war, there are few signs of conflict. My best photo of the day happens as I drop by the station to buy tram tickets. A small group of forlorn women surrounded by bags are waiting for a train. I photograph them from a distance, then make eye contact and move closer as they start feeding pigeons. Georgio, 17-year-old soldier also waiting for a train, translates my inadequate attempts at conversation. Basilica and Maria have lost their homes and are off to relatives in Rijeka. Fortified by drink, one minute they are crying, the next, laughing at their plight.

>> Brazda Camp, Macedonia, April 20th 1999

The day starts with early breakfast with Japanese tourists in Thessaloniki, then a Mercedes taxi ride to the border. Walk across, and another taxi is waiting, as arranged – emails have made the logistics of travelling so easy. Sasha takes me to the Care office in Skopje, and ten minutes later I am driving to the largest camp for Kosovan refugees, Brazda, just on the edge of town. All the TV images are there right in front of me – a mass of humanity on the move. Am in the middle of Europe with the dispossessed, a three-hour drive from the splendours of the ruins of ancient civilisation.

>>> UAE Camp, Kukes, Albania, May 19th 1999

Women who had washing machines at home are managing with buckets and bowls – endless washing because of a) living in mud and b) everyone has few clothes. The 'arab' camp is the most desirable – chicken for lunch instead of pasta. Those not allowed in come and take tea through the fence.

Kolosok Camp, Ingushetia,
June 10th 2000

Even an old cowshed has become home to refugees:
the animals have one half, and Chechens the other.

> Kolosok Camp, Ingushetia, June 10th 2000

In the garden a tent pitched under the mulberry trees
serves as a school. A small group of children are
eagerly learning Russian – their passport to a future.
The beautiful young refugee teacher in a black swishing
skirt and low-cut pink top painstakingly helps them form
letters. She's divorced, had to leave her son with her
husband and is grateful to be out working rather than
cooped up with her strict father. Frustrated at the
inactive life of the refugee, he takes it out on her.

**Clissold Park, North London, UK,
November 30th 1997**

Mimi looks like one of many young mothers playing with her children in the park, but she's also an Algerian journalist seeking asylum in Britain. Since the 1991 elections, when the army stepped in when it looked like the FIS (Islamic Salvation Front) might win, around 100,000 people have died violent deaths. Journalists were particularly vulnerable, especially if they tried to expose the perpetrators. Life became too dangerous for Mimi in Algeria and with her journalist husband and children she fled to Britain. Her future is uncertain as she waits for her case to be heard.

**> National Workshop Camp, Freetown,
Sierra Leone, October 13th 1999**

Displaced families live in an old engine repair shed. Even though the war is ostensibly over, thousands of people have no home to return to.

Peshawar, Pakistan, December 12th 2001

I go to visit an Afghan refugee camp, an hour's drive
from Peshawar, just one of the many that house the
million plus Afghans who have sought asylum in
Pakistan. Vibrant pinks and bright greens, long braids
with coloured tassels and men in richly embroidered
hats mark these as people from the Turkmenistan
border. They've been here for ten years and have a
tranquil village of sculpted mud houses. They were
doing OK, weaving carpets at home. Latifa still does
so with her daughter Arzi, but she is doubtful whether
they will find a market for their beautiful intricate
handicraft. Since September 11th 2001, the market
for carpets has disappeared. The home-workers are
destitute, they look as though they are starving.

> Bogota, Colombia, March 17th 2000

In the centre of the city a group of indigenous people –
the Embera Katio – have been camping for four months
in front of the Ministry of the Environment to protest
against the loss of their ancestral lands to a
hydroelectric scheme. Living under black plastic, they

make jewellery to earn some cash, and have organised
school classes for the children, but when it rains, as it
did last night, everything gets soaked and everyone
coughs.

>> Beach Camp, Gaza, October 25th 2000

Possibly the best located refugee camp in the world –
sitting beside the Mediterranean. The downside –
almost one million refugees live in Gaza in poor housing.
The environment, chronic unemployment and the stress
of constant conflict have had a devastating effect on the
mental health of women, especially the mothers of
sons. When boys go out to play they could be down at
the beach, or up at the checkpoint throwing stones and
courting death.

A group of physiotherapy students earnestly make notes, then get on with their busy clinic at the ICRC (International Committee for the Red Cross/Crescent) Orthopaedic Centre in Kabul. The first time I met their teacher, in 1996, she too was a student. It's great to see Rohafza running the unit now and we chat as she fits a new prosthesis for Nafas Gul.

Like everyone who works in the centre, Rohafza also has a disability. 'I've been a physiotherapist for eight years. When I was a medical student I came here to get my prosthesis changed and asked about jobs. At the time they were looking for a female physiotherapist so they took me on and sent me for training. When I was eleven I was injured by a mine explosion in the playground at school – I lost my leg above the knee. During the Taliban we were able to continue working here inside the centre although as soon as we went outside we had problems. We couldn't go out without a male blood relative, and there were no other jobs available to women. We had a lot of problems with the chadori (burqas). If you are disabled it's very difficult to control it, to make sure your face or leg isn't showing. I'm the only breadwinner in my family. My father is unemployed – he was a driver in the university but since it was closed he has had no work. I support ten people. I'm the eldest – my brothers and sisters are all at school. I'm not sure how the future will be. We're hoping for peace. My job is great because I am helping disabled people. In Afghanistan there is a lot of prejudice against them. When a woman loses a leg in a mine or rocket accident, then the husband looks for a new wife.'

ICRC Orthopaedic Centre, Kabul, Afghanistan, December 2nd 2001

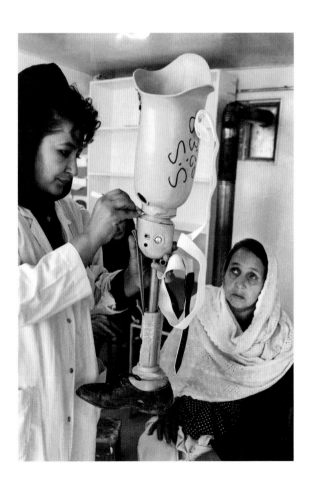

Cité Soleil, Haiti, December 30th 1991

Get taxi out to sprawling Cité Soleil, an enormous
shanty town on the outskirts of the city. A 'guide',
Régale, attaches himself to us and then becomes
very controlling on the photo front. In between
fearful moments I manage a few reasonable photos
but desperately want to meet women – all the macho
posturing on the street gets to me, as does the
stench of open sewers. Diving into a hairdresser's is
the best I can do, a different world to the street –
camaraderie of women, joking and laughing in spite
of dire economic situation – the post coup embargo is
making life impossible.

Kabul, Afghanistan, August 2nd 1988

6.30 a.m. – with our all-women film crew (plus two
minders) across the already wide-awake bustling city
to a messy factory which makes prefabricated sections
of houses – these will become six-storey blocks of flats
for workers – very much in the Soviet style. (Eight years
later these blocks are in a dreadful state, bombed and
shelled, whole walls are missing. They look totally bleak.
No running water – children have to fetch endless
buckets from the pump.) The workers are all women or
old men – since all the younger men have been called
up by the Soviet backed government to fight the CIA
backed mujahadeen. Complete lack of safety regulations
– the factory floor a mess of writhing lengths of wire.
Noisy, dirty and sweaty. Great woman crane driver who
giggles and smokes, and takes enormous pleasure in
her elevated position. Endless taking off and landing of
helicopters – Soviet troops have only a few weeks
before the deadline for withdrawal.

> Adwa, Ethiopia, March 2nd 1994

98th anniversary of the battle of Adwa, where the
Ethiopians defeated the Italian army. Early morning
drive there, only to find nothing is happening, so drink
tea and visit the market. Most activity around the
grinding mill – a fitting symbol of women's work.

< Kabul, Afghanistan, March 17th 1996

To the miserable Indira Gandhi hospital – freezing and filthy. In the children's ward a whole group of children with mine injuries, including seven-year-old Tariq, watched over by his fearful mother, Sherifa. Three days ago he thought he saw a plastic pen and picked it up. It exploded – he lost one hand, injured the other and his body. Now Sherifa has a disabled child to care for on top of all her other problems.

< Port au Prince, Haiti, December 30th 1991

'La reve du peuple c'est complètement égaté'
(the dream of the people is completely spoilt) says the
hotel security guard. Lots of mosquitoes, no water or
electricity, dog fights all night. Post coup Haiti feels very
insecure. Mango for breakfast, then get ride to Canadian
Embassy where press corps have gathered because of
rumours that the 17 young men who have occupied it,
are going to be leaving at 9 a.m. By 12 nothing has
happened, apart from Red Cross negotiator appearing –
an incongruously smart woman surrounded by heavily
armed guards.

Orota, Eritrea, March 26th 1988

In the middle of the night (once the generators can
safely run without attracting the attention of surveillance
planes) visit a series of hidden containers which turn out
to be a pharmaceutical production line. Workers are
masked and dressed in white, hard to believe we're in
the middle of a war zone. Making aspirin, tetracycline,
anti-histamine and iv fluid packs – this unit supplies the
adjoining underground hospital and 50% of Eritrea's
drug needs.

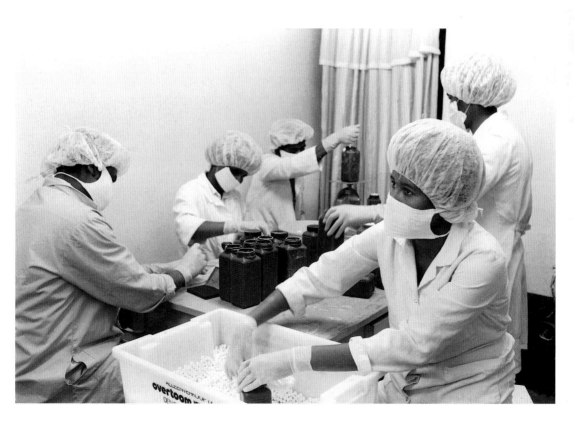

< Suchitoto, El Salvador, May 7th 1986

An eerie drive along blasted roads, navigating road-blocks of rocks and strips of asphalt, all the houses bombed out, graffiti – 'Yanquis fuera de El Salvador'. To celebrate the Day of the Soldier a dance is going on in one of the bars – smoochy music in the afternoon, not enough girls to go round. Ask to take photos – told OK as long as I don't misrepresent the situation. Where does misrepresentation begin and end?

> San Salvador, El Salvador, November 15th 1990

Women still shop and keep things ticking over in spite of the civil war.

>> Butare, Rwanda, December 14th 1995

Another children's centre. Here nuns are caring for those separated from their parents during the genocide, or the flight to Zaire. Surviving family members visit and mournfully inspect the children, looking for familiar faces.

>>> Butare, Rwanda, December 13th 1995

With Save the Children social workers to persuade foster families to give up children to be reunited with their families (delicate work – some families have taken in children to get free farm labour). Twenty-one-year-old Césarie is caring, diplomatic and forceful. First have to get letter from local bourgemeistre (the town official) then long, long drive. First meet elder son Damian, who says dad isn't at home – see the child we've come for – Uwimana – in very dirty tattered clothes playing in a banana plantation. After persistent asking, the foster father, Simon, does appear. Says the child has to be washed – fears that the child will disappear but in fact reappears after 10 minutes, sparkling and in very clean clothes. Simon, in spite of looking like Mr Hard, seems genuinely sorry to be handing him over.

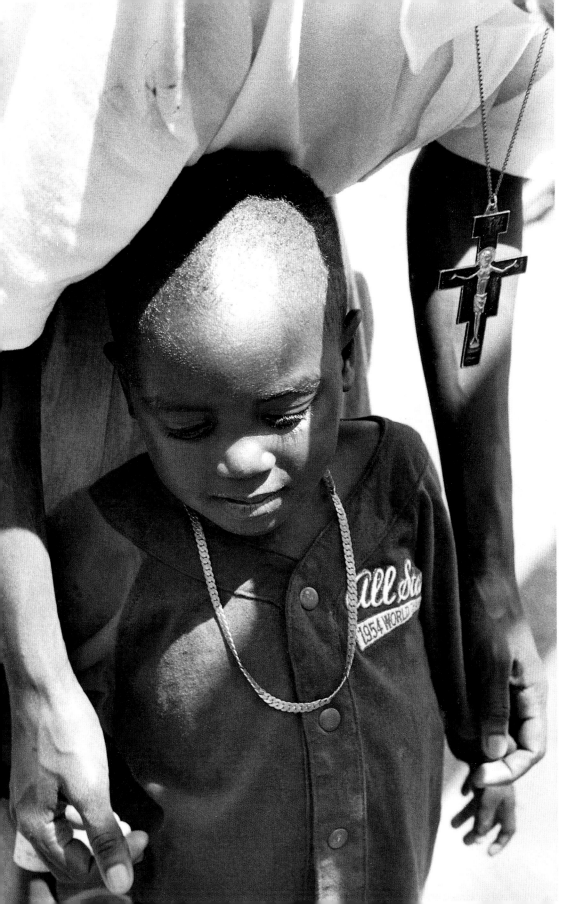

Comayaguela, Honduras, November 4th 1985

Wander around seedy area of town, working girls hanging around the doorways of cheap hotels. Share cigarettes and chat to 16-year-old Martine, very sad and worldly wise, with no hopes for the future. 'I was sold into a brothel near the US base. We earnt $20 a time from the soldiers, but I never saw the money because the woman bought me clothes, make-up and food, so my debt got bigger and bigger. I was picked up by the police because I was under-age, and had to come back here. We earn ten lempira a day here, and the room costs two.' A slobbery guy appears, touching up women as he passes them.

> Near Sisak, Croatia, December 3rd 1991

Drive back from frontline towards Sisak, stopping to photograph Marisa beating the hell out of her washing in the freezing mist, mortars booming in the background.

Maganja da Costa, Mozambique, March 3rd 1989

Neighbouring villages have been captured by Renamo, the bandits, and people used as human shields to stop the army attacking, but still women go off to the rice fields to try to produce some food, wading through waist high water to get there. Everyone seems unnervingly jolly, singing, flirting, almost dancing as we walk back together.

> Freetown, Sierra Leone, October 10th 1999

I return to the amputee camp. A heartening place to visit because everyone makes you feel welcome, heart-rending because everyone has stories of absolute barbarity. At first I found it strange that all the people who had had limbs hacked off were housed in the same place, but it did mean it was easy to provide special training and medical facilities.

Meet Abu Bakarr Kargbo, a sad 25-year-old caring for his three-year-old daughter Yama and 9-month-old son, Abu Bakarr. He has a 19-year-old wife, Rugiatu, who cares for him as well as their neighbour, 72-year-old Nathaniel, whose wife was burnt to death inside their house before his leg was chopped off. Abu speaks of his wife with great love: 'My wife does everything for me – dressing me, washing me, giving me chop to eat. On 26th January 99 in the presence of my wife and daughter my arms were chopped off. Rugiatu gives me courage. Whatever I need she gives me. She never refuses me anything. Although I have lost my hands I have courage because of my wife and children. It makes me not consider my problem too much. I was a builder – I can do nothing again.'

Pristina, Kosovo, January 9th 1993

A brief respite from fear and trepidation on street –
to a home where it's bride's night – tomorrow Luminje
will be married. Her matron of honour and attendants,
all dressed in white and gold, stand very seriously
clutching embroidered hankies. The room full of women
have soft drinks or tea, dance, giggle and chat.

> Baghdad, Iraq, November 16th 1999

In a poor part of Saddam City visit a school for
children with hearing problems. Surprised by order and
calm – the teachers have been on a course and are
keen to show off their new skills. Could be anywhere
in the world.

>> Grozny, Chechnya, June 7th 2000

Food distribution. A young girl hangs on to her
grandmother, the traditional carer world-wide.

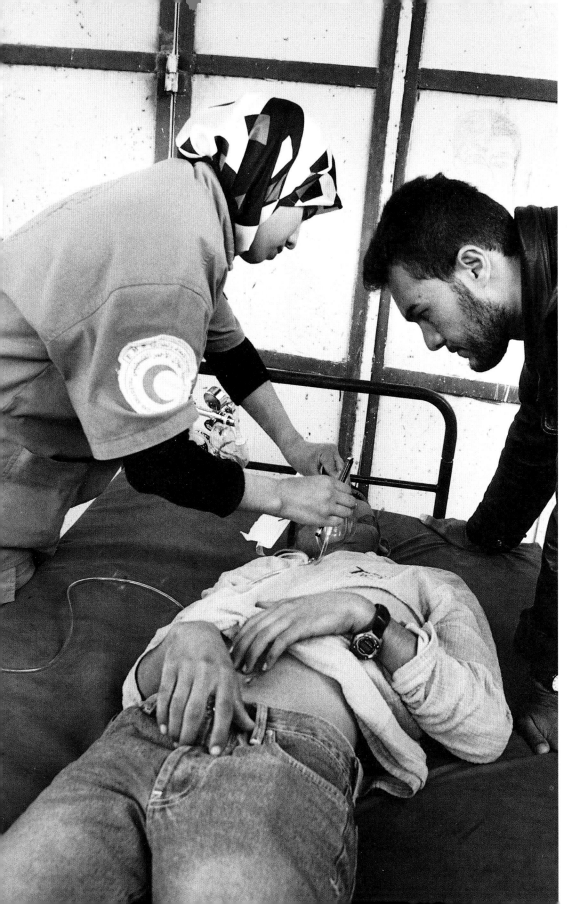

<< Gaza, October 24th 2000

Mid afternoon to the Israel border checkpoint: youths are throwing stones, soldiers are shooting back, the Red Crescent have set up a field hospital in a garage – several ambulances screech in at the same time – triage system, lots of tear gas inhalation. One boy, shot in the stomach, has massive internal bleeding and dies as he's put in the ambulance.

< Gaza, April 10th 2002

Nadia Shaath has come to the beauty salon for a pedicure, manicure, make-up and hair-do because this afternoon she's getting married.

'I was going to marry Karim 10 days ago but because the Israelis occupied Ramallah we had to postpone it. I wanted to wait longer but was worried that the situation might get even worse so we've gone ahead with it. I've three friends who are also getting married today. Because Colin Powell is coming this week we think things will probably be alright whilst he is here. Our wedding is at 5 p.m., much earlier than normal because it is dangerous for people to travel after dark. We also have to have it discreetly. It will be in a restaurant, but with the curtains closed because with such a sad situation it's not good to have a showy wedding. Lots of friends who I'd like to have at my wedding can't come because they can't travel.

My future husband is an engineer but he has been laid off from his work with a construction company because of the uncertain situation. We don't know what the future holds.'

> Kabul, Afghanistan, December 2nd 2001

In the rambling city market people bring odd possessions to try to sell and raise enough cash to get through another week. Market business is traditionally done by men, widows have no choice but to take their place alongside them. Taking photographs is pretty tricky, as a large gawking crowd of young boys gathers as soon as a camera appears. Even envy women wearing burqas for the anonymity they confer.

>> Kabul, Afghanistan, December 5th 2001

Go along to a distribution to widows of non-food items by Care. Everyone is very good-humoured – just as well as they have to spend hours being registered and lining up to be given blankets, buckets, soap etc. Before the Taliban took over the government in 1996, food distributions were a regular feature of life for widows. Even when women couldn't go out, the workers visited them at home.

Ma'aza The fighter

I met Ma'aza, a veteran fighter, as she was recovering in hospital from a miscarriage. In spite of being in pain she insisted on talking. Many Eritrean women fighters put off having children until the war was over, but then found it was hard to find a partner. Men preferred submissive domesticated wives rather than feisty independent women.

'The political struggle for Eritrean women started in the 1950s. I joined in September 1974 – then there were just five women fighters. Some of the men encouraged us to participate but for the majority it was difficult for them to understand about equality or women. They said, "How can women climb mountains?" Amongst the men, though, there were a few who encouraged us and said women must be equal. We knew that when there was a battle we would prove ourselves – we would either fight or die. There were a few women who had already been fighting – they told us that not only was the battle hard but there was also hunger – only leaves to eat. We were encouraged to be in front – and we really thought we would die. I can't lie and say I understood the politics – I was only 13 – but what pushed us on was seeing the Ethiopians killing women in front of us. Seeing them cut off women's breasts. This made us leave home to fight. My parents were crying, but they couldn't do anything about it. Before I joined up, I hadn't travelled at all, and I hadn't seen anything of the war.

Being a fighter was hard – hunger, travelling on foot for days on end with nothing in your stomach – some days we couldn't even find water. When the battle came it was a relief – you felt that if you died that would be a relief, a rest. Up until 1976 we were actually fighting Eritreans, because the commanders in the Ethiopian army were Eritrean and they knew the land. There was one girl who was surrounded by six Ethiopians, they were laughing and saying it's only a girl. She knew the only way out of the situation was to kill someone – she got a hand grenade ready – when five of them came for her she threw it, and killed all six.

Although we were dying alongside the men, we still weren't taken seriously by some of them. One woman even killed herself because she was given such a hard time. Late in 1975, there were more women joining the field and by then there was war throughout the country. There was no solution. Women showed they could do everything and from then on we were encouraged. The men stopped questioning what we were doing – in some areas the leaders were two women instead of three boys.
We still have to struggle for equality for women – in the countryside many women are in the same position as before. As a mother I'd feel sorry if my daughter went off to fight, but if there's no other solution they have to join up.'

Eritrea, May 14th 1995

Managua, Nicaragua, April 18th 1982

In sweltering heat a group of volunteers, half of them women, have turned up for militia training, learning how to clean and assemble rifles, how to shoot without actually firing.

> Matagalpa, Nicaragua, November 12th 1985

Driving back from photographing coffee pickers, lots of soldiers on the road, including 14-year-old Marta, hot and sweaty in her uniform. She's been in the reserve for a year, serious and childish in her shyness – makes me feel frivolous.

Managua, Nicaragua, November 5th 1984
Wander down to the post office, now guarded by
two militia members – a man in uniform and Martha
Lorena, in high heels, with carefully varnished fingers
cradling her gun.

> San Jose las Flores, El Salvador, April 27th 1989
After hassles of getting safe-conduct signed by
colonel, eventually set off. Idyllic village scenes of
ploughing and hammock-weaving put into context of

the war with the buzz of circling helicopters. Arrive at
San Jose as compas are coming in from the hills – 13-
year-old radio operator Delme is supremely confident.

>> Guatemala City, September 5th 1985
Small skirmishes across the city – some market sellers
who decided to strike in support of the students' strike
are arrested for their pains and unceremoniously
thrown into the back of an army truck.

< Guatemala City, September 6th 1985

Coffee at Patisseria Austriana, one of the bizarre
delights of the city, then wander off to find action.
Municipality is on strike, police everywhere with riot
shields and gas canisters. Find crowd of indigenous
women in front of law courts, members of the GAM
(Grupo de Apoyo Mutuel, the support group for the
disappeared). Large banner unfurled with the names of
the missing, threatening presence of police.

Women go into Supreme Court and occupy it for an
hour. Lots of skirmishes on the street, speculation that
there's lots of provocation going on. An anarchic band
of kids trash the gas station, break windscreens and
shop windows – army dons gas masks and suddenly
opens fire ... starts hosing people down with tear gas,
crowd disperses, a running mass of people.

Puerto Cortes, Honduras, August 25th 1983

Press call for arrival of USS *Nassau*, part of US army
manoeuvres.* Fifty women stevedores are part of the
team. Strong women, proud of the job they do,
although none of the US soldiers seems to know why
they are here, or is able to question the role of the
American army in Central America.

(*Nicaragua thought this was a warm up for an
invasion. In fact in December US troops went into
Grenada.)

> Solomana Camp, Eritrea, March 25th 1988

As it begins to get dark, we drive up to some thorn
bushes at the foot of steep stony hills. Looking closer,
realise it's a classroom, carefully hidden. Women are
learning to read and write in the midst of a war – the
Kalashnikov in the front row is the only sign that this is
not a normal evening class.

Afabet, Eritrea, March 28th 1988

After driving all night come to the battlefield –
apocalyptic scene of burnt-out tanks ambushed in a
narrow valley. Dead Ethiopian soldiers are everywhere –
the Eritreans claim they put out of action three divisions
and a mechanised brigade – in human terms that's
18,000 troops killed, captured or forced to flee. One poor
man has virtually melted into the asphalt. Back at the
base, fighters are relaxing after last week's battle.

Afghanistan, August 3rd 1988

Hanging out in hillside village, drinking tea.
Suddenly group of militia appear, mostly women, pause for a photo opportunity, then disappear. Turns out they are the defence for the village. With mujahadeen closing in on Kabul, and Soviet army about to withdraw, everyone is a bit nervous about the future.
With good reason. By the time I returned to Afghanistan in 1996 the Taliban controlled most of the country (including Kabul by September 1996). Women could no longer go out to work, sing, wear make-up or noisy shoes, let alone brandish guns and roam the countryside unveiled.

> Near Hebron, West Bank, June 30th 1990

Visit one of the women's committees – a mass of animated women packed into a room in the nursery they have set up – point out importance of a place to play peacefully for children who have lost so much of normal life with parents in prison, and the attraction of throwing stones and taking part in street protests.
The Intifada (uprising) has given women a new role, now they are leading demonstrations, and working. With so many men in prison, they have become financially responsible – the coops (bakeries, farms, etc.) set up by the women's committees, have made this possible.

>> Mbazi, Rwanda, June 22nd 1995

Lindsey (Hilsum) and I spend the morning trailing around small villages and checking out the huts at the back of the village halls – those accused of involvement in genocide are being held in these 'cachots'. We meet a woman accused of cutting open a dead woman and taking out her insides, another of betraying her neighbour and handing over children to the Hutu militia. Tanazia is a Hutu villager confused by the accusations made against her. She was arrested with her husband who is accused of being among the killers. She's been locked up with the youngest of her five children, the rest have been left to take care of themselves.

<< Kigali prison, Rwanda, March 20th 1995

Nearly 8,000 prisoners in a prison built for 2,000 – of those, 260 are women accused of participation in the genocide, 194 are children, some detainees, others there because their mothers have no one else to care for them. The director, Frank Kalyamiti, is under pressure, 'Today I was lucky and no one died. The overcrowding is intolerable, the courts need to start working so we can set the innocent free. The military arrest them and just dump them here – these aren't prisoners, they are detainees, they haven't been before a magistrate yet. The prisons are very small and old – they were not built with genocide in mind.' Of course the women all protest their innocence, but from other testimonies it's clear women did take part in the killing. It's also clear though that old scores are being settled.

< Greenham Common, UK, May 12th 1984

Rebecca is arrested after cutting the fence in a protest over the presence of cruise missiles on the US base.

> Sisak cemetery, Croatia, December 3rd 1991

... to the cemetery, surreal sight of gun emplacement behind newly dug graves. Meet Nevenka, single mother of two teenagers. Proud of her anti-aircraft gun. Team a bit shaken as bomb had landed there earlier in the afternoon.

Leave them in gathering gloom to drive back to town to get film processed before the Happy Snaps in Zagreb closes – and to eat pizza – disconcerting that life goes on normally a short drive away.

> Road from Split to Tuzla, Bosnia, December 5th 1994

Drive through a landscape of destruction. Twenty-year-old Rocio, a Spanish soldier serving with the UN, is on traffic duty, waving vehicles, mostly Red Cross convoys, across a narrow bridge.

>> East Jerusalem, October 27th 2000

There's a heavy security presence at Damascus Gate as young men are barred from going to the Al Aqsa mosque for Friday prayers. They set up their 'prayer mats' (mostly bits of old cardboard) in the road and pray with a gentle rain falling, then march between Herod and Damascus Gates followed by police on horses. Many young women soldiers, mostly watching and chatting. Lots of anger but after a while everyone goes off for lunch.

Consolée The survivor

In a small shack amongst sweet potato fields I meet Consolée Mukakalisa. 'The life we lead is a miserable one. My handicap prevents me from doing anything whatsoever, I am completely destroyed, unable to even cook. I am a young girl of 23 years. I knew how to write and I used to get along fine before the genocide. I managed to survive, but what can I do now?
When Habyarimana was killed (the Rwandan President's plane was shot down on April 6th 1994, an event which sparked off the genocide), I went to visit my grandmother. The tragedy did not take place immediately; we had to wait a week and a half for things to get really bad.
On the morning of 18th April 1994, there was a feeling of panic in the Tutsi community. Everyone was looking for a place to hide. I preferred to go into the forest nearby but the criminals found me that very day. There were a lot of men, women, girls and boys who were practically all Hutus from the area and they all supported the Tutsi genocide. They put me in the front of a vehicle and drove me to the Rinda road. When we got there, they undressed

me. They gave my clothes to a woman who was taking part in this attack. They hit me several times with their machetes and this is how my right hand was cut off as well as the fingers from my left hand apart from the thumb. I was also hit on the head and on the left leg with machetes and then I fell unconscious to the ground. This was at about 10 a.m.

That evening I regained consciousness. I was completely soaked because it had been raining a lot. I was so thirsty that I drank the rainwater from the ponds. I tried to get up, but it was impossible. How can you get up without hands? I dragged myself along the ground. When I arrived at my grand-mother's house, I found it had been already destroyed. I stayed amongst the ruins. I did not see anyone. I spent the night there bleeding profusely.

The next day, the criminals returned. They looked at me but did not have the compassion to finish me off! On the contrary, they said that I should be left to die of my injuries. I stayed there. My nourishment was rainwater. I began to decompose because of my untreated wounds.

Three days later, I was attacked again by a man called Nyaminani and an old man. Nyaminani hit me with a machete and the old man hit me on the head with a massue (a pounder). However I was still not dead. I begged them to finish me off but they refused. For the next few days I waited for death. However a Red Cross vehicle came and picked me up. It took me to the university hospital, because the Kibayi health centre had refused to look after me. They said I was too ill to be treated. At the university hospital I was treated once a week. It was useless in my case, because the soldiers kept on coming to take away the sick and kill them. They did it mostly at night. This discouraged the nurses who agreed to help us. The other nurses took sides with our killers. When the RPF (Rwandan Patriotic Force) took over the country, I stayed at the university hospital until July this year.'

Butare, Rwanda, December 18th 1995

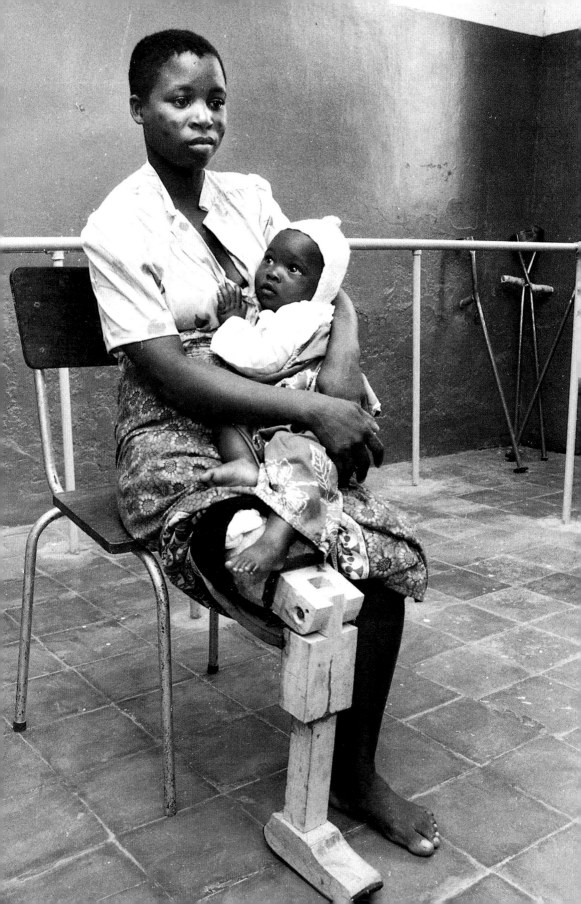

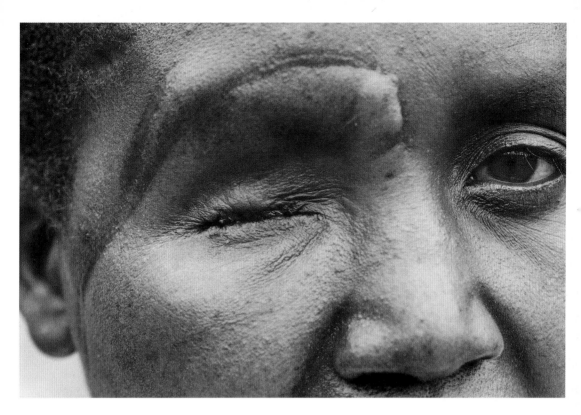

< Quelimane, Mozambique, February 27th 1989

With International Red Cross delegate to the hospital annexe that fits artificial legs for those who stepped on landmines, and survived. Meet a group who are waiting for their legs to be cast – first the stump is measured, then a mould of it is made in plaster, next the lower leg and foot are made in wood. This all takes about a month – so people from villages have to be pretty determined. First just to get to Quelimane. In a country with no roads or transport, apart from the odd tractor, walking is the only option. Then they have to stick around waiting for the prosthesis to be made. Zaina Jose is from Pebane. She's 19, her baby son, six months old. She stepped on a mine last year.

Butare, Rwanda, December 18th 1995

Christine Mukamuera: '...a man called Ndejeje came towards me and asked me to give him some money. I said I didn't have any. He told me to hold out my hands and say that Kagame (leader of the Rwandan Patriotic Front) had lied to us. I did it. Then he hit me on my right eye with the machete and my left hand was cut off. He also hit me on my head and I lost consciousness. This was at about 9 a.m. and I came around at about 5 p.m. I noticed that my baby was covered in mud and blood.'

< Karte-se hospital, Kabul, March 12th 1996

'There's a lot of surviving, not much living in Kabul', a friend says as we sip tea. The ICRC hospital, which specialises in war wounded, bears this out. Wards full of people with bits missing. Then come across Bilqis – injured by a rocket two years ago. She has come for a stump revision and beams with vitality.

Ganda, Angola, February 27th 1997

In a lush back garden find 14-year-old Evalina Janete, a victim of both sides of the war. 'In 1993 I was kidnapped by Unita and taken to Casseque. There was a mortar attack by the MPLA (government forces) and I was injured – there was an unbearable pain in my arm. With peace a man from my village came to get me and took me to hospital, and there they amputated my arm.'

< Piscina Camp, Tirana, Albania, June 22nd 1999

Go to Family Planning Association to meet Valentina ... who has been organising counselling and, if wanted, abortions for women raped in Kosovo. She starts off by saying the whole population has been raped, pointing out the difficulty of differentiating between a woman who has been raped, lost a child, lost part of her body, and the mental anguish everyone is going through. Valentina sends me off to one of the city's refugee camps with a young student, Blerta, who visits women in the camp who have asked for help. The camp is in the grounds of the outdoor swimming pool and the tents make it look like a holiday camp in the sunshine, but behind every tent flap are innumerable tragedies. With a common language, Blerta fits in really well with the young Kosovan girls. Given the enormous amount of cultural and family pressure on women not to talk about what has happened, it's really impressive the trust that she has established.

Port au Prince, Haiti, October 20th 1998

I meet Financia, getting ready to go to school, a new experience for the shy ten year old who until recently was a 'restavek', a virtual slave, sent by her family to do domestic work in the city, in return for a bed and food. Financia has been taken in by Kayfam (a centre which gives help to victims of domestic violence) after a neighbour, passing the house, saw her bound hand and foot to a bed and being raped by the 'master' – something which the little girl says happened regularly. The centre would like to return her to her family, but Financia has no idea where she comes from.

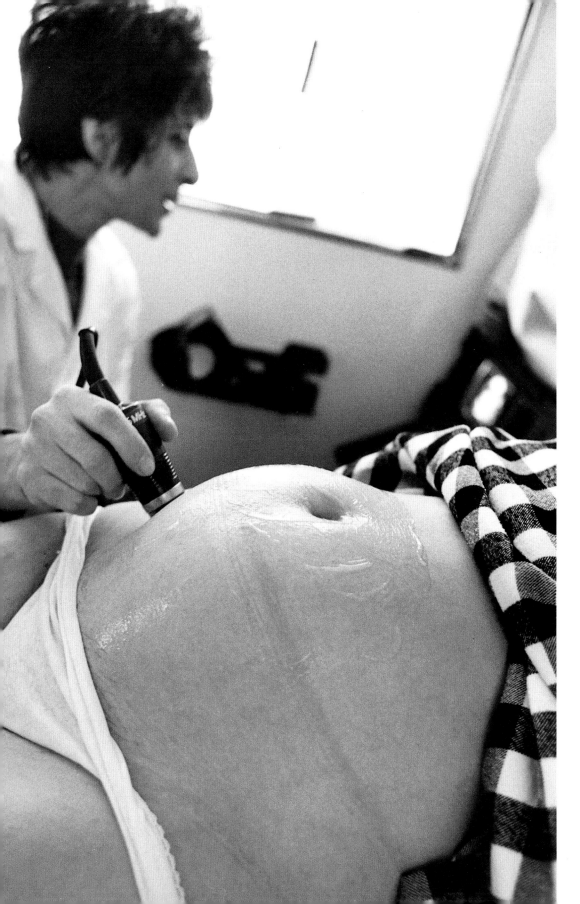

Near Tuzla, Bosnia, December 6th 1994

Travel with an ambulance that has been converted into a mobile gynaecological clinic and the volunteer doctor and nurses from Tuzla hospital who work in it. The unit was set up by Care Austria as a discreet way of treating women who had been violated and traumatised in the course of the war. The Bosnian Ministry of Health estimates 30,000 women have been abused during the war, but most hide what happened to them. As Muslim women it's hard to talk about sex and rape. So far the doctor says she has seen eight pregnant girls from the concentration camps where they were repeatedly raped by the Serbs – six have had abortions and two have had their babies.

Drive through slushy snow to an ugly sprawling village. Immediately surrounded by a large group of women who have been waiting for the mobile clinic.

First everyone is given a questionnaire to fill out – asking about their background, if they are displaced, have experienced violence, if they use contraception,

how they feel about their experiences. Everyone fills it in very painstakingly, many are not used to reading and writing. Eventually a queue forms to see the doctor. Today most of the women say they have come for contraception – until the war, abortion was the most common way of limiting the number of babies a woman had. Besides the practical care of smears, pregnancy tests, ultrasound and contraception there is also a back-up psychotherapy team who can provide counselling. Dr Vesnic explains the high number of sexually transmitted diseases, pointing out the lack of water and difficulty of keeping clean. Also there's a lot more sex going on, as there's little else to do. Move on to refugee camp for next visit – here the confidence and trust the women have in the clinic prompt them to ask shyly if it's possible to have a special place for couples because living up to 20 people in a room makes sex difficult. The clinic has been a great success because reproductive health is a problem for everyone, particularly in a time of disruption.

Gulu, Uganda, March 16th 1999

Go to meet Grace and her sick baby in a little shack on the edge of town. She was 13 and in the third year of primary school when she was abducted from her boarding school by the Lord's Resistance Army – Unicef estimates 15,000 children have been kidnapped over the last decade. Many of the girls had been forced to live with the soldiers as extra wives, in effect sex slaves. It's just a year since she managed to escape from her captors, running away whilst there was a battle going on between them and the Ugandan army. When she was brought to Gulu she kept being sick and didn't know why until the nurse told her she was pregnant. She had been the 'wife' of a commander, 'I have no feelings for him', she says by way of polite understatement.

Grace lives with her four-month-old baby in a one-room house rented by her parents, who have been very supportive, unlike many who see their children as collaborators with the enemy and a source of shame. She has called her daughter Hope.

> Outskirts of Kampala, Uganda, June 14th 1991

a.m. – nurses training-course on the psychological and social effects of war – around half a million people were killed in Uganda in the early 1980s and a lot of medical problems can be traced back to that violence – it's an eye-opener for most of the new students to discover mental as well as physical effects of war.

p.m. to the edge of town. A group of 15 or so women sit on a veranda making beautifully bright woven mats while they wait their turn to see the nurse for counselling. The women are all victims of torture. This is the practical part of the nurses' training. In Ugandan culture, it's an insult directly to ask a woman about rape so they are taught to look for symptoms – feelings of guilt (maybe the wife survived while her husband was killed), apathy, listlessness. All the women wear traditional costume – six metres of cloth wrapped around with butterfly-wing sleeves. They manage to smile and laugh together, a small respite.

Freetown, Sierra Leone, October 17th 1999

16-year-old Adamasy Bangura calmly describes the loss of her child: 'We were living in a small village in Port Loko district when rebels attacked us. This was in February 1998. It was day-time and we tried to run away but I was unfortunate to be captured. They brought me to the village. I was holding my two-year-old baby boy. First they killed him with an axe. I cried "Where is my baby, oh my baby", so they hit me with a cutlass (machete) on my head. There is a deep scar there. After that they asked me to put my hand on a stick which was on the ground and they chopped at my right hand. Then they ran away and left me. I tried to go into the bush to find my mother who was hiding there. Luckily I found her and my father and my brothers. They were all in the bush. They took me to the next village – Madina. My hand hadn't been completely chopped so the doctor at Kambia, Dr Koroma, amputated it. Then I was brought to Connaught hospital. I spent four days there then I was discharged and went to stay with my mother in Freetown.

We were living there until January this year, but then on the 6th the house was burnt down by rebels and that's how I ended up here in the Amputee Camp, together with four members of my family who don't have anywhere else to go. It's hard to find a boyfriend when your hand has been cut. My hope is to be able to have a small business like a shop.'

In the amputee camp Fina Kamara is busy weeding her sweet potato patch, one of the few amputees who is determined to use her artificial hand.

'My hand was chopped off by rebels from the former Sierra Leonean army – the junta – in May 97 when they began cutting hands. I'm a farmer so I was working on the farm in the morning, planting groundnuts. Just after I left the farm I was cutting some sweet potato leaves to cook for my children. As I left I heard some firing in the town and at first I thought it was ECOMOG, the West African peace-keeping mission, but then there was an ambush and I couldn't escape. There were about nine of us caught and chopped – about ten people were killed. My sister and her husband were amongst those killed. My grandfather died in the bush that night. His hand had been chopped, it was raining and the pain was too much for him.'

< Magoro Camp, Katakwi, Uganda, December 12th 2002

Travelling round these camps created out of conflict, I meet a stream of HIV positive women, living in poverty and all anxious about what the future holds for their children, and concerned at how to survive and fight the virus.

Florence Tino, is the mother of four. 'My husband died in March 2002, and he was positive. I know I am as well. My husband left me five cows but they were taken by raiders in July. My relatives were looking after them in Ocorimongin Camp when it was attacked. I've lost my husband, my home, my wealth but I try to avoid gloomy thoughts as I have to bring up my children. If I think of how bad things are I'll lose weight, and I need to be strong. There's no one else to care for the children.

Since I have been here in the camp I've had no garden (to grow food). I tried ploughing some land nearby and planted groundnuts but they dried up and died. I just go and assist others and they give me something or I go and cry at my sister but I can't keep on doing that. I'm feeding the children bitter greens. They are in school – I can't afford to buy them uniforms but the teacher lets them go anyway. I don't have a partner at the moment but I'm experiencing such stages of poverty you never know what the future holds for us – I'm resisting finding another husband and having more children but overnight you can find yourself in a net, things happen.'

> Kabul, Afghanistan, December 8th 2001

In the car park of the Red Cross centre a woman is quietly crying to herself, half-heartedly trying to amuse her baby. I smile, she smiles, she introduces 18-month-old Ailsian and then starts chattering in broken English, 'I'm Hazara, we have many problems, we're very poor. I'm looking for a hospital for nervous diseases – I think I'm crazy, I can't cope any more, my husband has no job, I have no job, I just cry. I was educated, I can speak some English, but what can I do. I need some help.'

Laura   The widow

I'm warmly welcomed at the Mothers' Committee. They show me their albums – incredible that a photographer goes out and takes pictures when bodies are found (often on the rubbish dump), and then the relatives of 'the disappeared' can come to the office and look for missing family members. Laura Pinto, one of the co-ordinators pours out her life.

'The Comite de Madres Monsenor Romero was set up in 1977. Two years earlier a student demonstration took place in the centre of town. Soldiers opened fire and hundreds of young people were killed or disappeared. Mothers of these young people went to the security forces, to the prisons and to government departments to get an answer to what had happened to their children – but they were never given any. In this way these mothers came together. When they went to the police headquarters they met other mothers and in 1977 a group decided to go to the Archbishop, Monsenor Romero, to ask for support. He told us to unite and form one voice. So on December 24th 1977 the Mothers' Committee was set up with three objectives – unconditional freedom for political prisoners, information about the disappeared and punishment for those who had assassinated our relations. We got together all legal resources that we could, but all we got from the security forces was threats at gun-point. They told us to go off and look in the mountains (implying they were with the guerrillas), or maybe they had gone off with other women. They threatened us and told us not to come back or we would be killed or disappeared.

Members of the committee have been arrested, tortured and raped. They want to know who are the leaders, but we don't have leaders, we work in commissions. There are around 500 mothers in the committee. For security reasons we aren't all here because, as you can see, there are heavily armed men all around the building. Here in our offices in San Salvador every day people come with their testimonies. We say we won't cry any more. We'll fight so that we win what we want – peace and equality. I'm here in the Mothers' Committee because in 1978 my "companera de vida" was arrested. He was a trade unionist in a sugar refinery. They were on strike asking for a wages rise and better conditions. I was at the factory gate trying to see what had happened because he hadn't come home. I found him with the security forces ready to shoot. When I went up to ask what was happening, why had he been arrested, a Colonel in the National Police put a machine gun to my chest and told me not to take another step. I argued with him and said he could kill me but I was doing absolutely nothing. As I argued people gathered round and took me away because it looked as though this man really wanted to machine gun me.

Whilst the men were being rounded up they kept asking who the leader was, and since my companero had a megaphone, they insisted he was. Twenty men, including him, were taken to one side. Then at 8 p.m. the families were told to come and see them, but some were missing. We went to the colonel. He said they would be investigated and freed the next day. That was a lie. We know that when people are picked up they don't reappear. The colonel told us the union leaders were terrorists and told us to go home. At 2 a.m. the 20 were taken off by the National Guard. At first we didn't know where they were but one of them had a relation, a colonel, and he told the family they were at the National Guard Barracks. They were brutally tortured. After eight days they were sent to the Penal Centre at Santa Tecla. Fifteen days later they were taken to Santa Ana. Four months later to San Vicente.

Thank God that I was helped by the Mothers' Committee. They denounced the case and six months later the 20 trade unionists were freed. During this time the Mothers helped me both economically and morally. I have four children and no way of maintaining them or visiting my husband.

Unfortunately my husband was assassinated in 1980. On June 20th some men dressed in civilian clothes came and got him. He was at home because he was out of work. Here, once you've been arrested it's impossible to carry on living in the country because you're labelled a terrorist and no one will give you work ... your name and identity card number are on a list. When they asked if he was at home, I said yes because we didn't have anything to hide. They said that they had to take him away for an investigation and that he'd be back the next day. Then I went looking for him with the two eldest children. I went to the police, to all the security bodies, but they said no, he hasn't been arrested. Then on the Saturday a neighbour came by with a newspaper and said, "Look isn't this your husband, killed in a battle near Sonsonate?" I said it wasn't possible, but his name and identity number were there in the paper. I went to Sonsonate and found him about to be buried as an unknown person. At this time I was seven months pregnant and I couldn't take the body away, but I saw him. There was just one bullet, a 38. And his thumbs were tied behind his back.'

On May 6th 1986 Laura Pinto was abducted by unknown men. On May 8th she was found abandoned in a park in San Salvador with knife wounds in her abdomen. She had been raped and tortured. On the evening of May 28th she was abducted once more, this time by four armed men in plain clothes. Later it was acknowledged that she was being held at the Treasury Police headquarters.

San Salvador, El Salvador, October 5th 1985

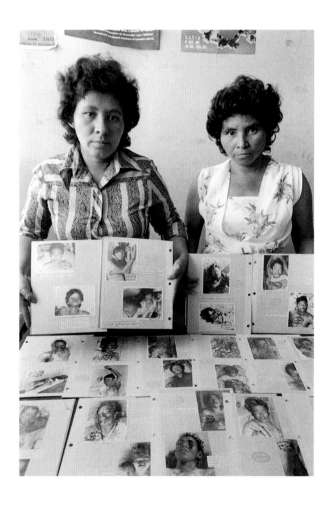

< Solola, Guatemala, September 23rd 1985

Drive past the village dormitories – everyone has to sleep there and be accounted for. Go to a rosary class – in the freezing cold, the widows sit attentively and clutch the new plastic rosaries that are handed out, seeking consolation in prayer.

San Marcos, Guatemala, September 10th 1985

Joan, a Mary Knoll sister, takes me to meet Justa, a feisty 73-year-old midwife and widow. She has recently discovered the pleasure of learning and is making the most of life. She insists on changing before any photos are taken and gets dressed up in her best huipil (decorated blouse) and silk corte (wrap-around skirt). Then we have to collect her sheep, and once she's found her hat, umbrella and shawl, is at last happy and ready.

< Kabul, Afghanistan, March 11th 1996

Huddle around the stove and the samovar is produced.
Razia, the only female chowkidar (caretaker) in Kabul,
stokes the fire and gets out her wedding photo – her
husband disappeared four years ago. In the photo
her hair is visible, and at 17 she is young and carefree.
She's only 32 now, but shrouded in black and living with
sadness, looks much older. She has three children and
has had to sell her furniture to keep them fed. All over
the world widows clutch photos of those they have
lost, literally holding on to memories and lost lives.

Asmara, Eritrea, May 19th 1995

After the war with Ethiopia, Eritrea has 16,000
disabled fighters. In the centre of town 250 of them,
including 33 women, occupy an old army base.
Hkbeket Woldai is 31, she spent 14 years at the front
and her husband was also a fighter. For the past seven
years she has sat in her wheelchair whiling away the
days. Her husband was killed 12 years ago, just before
she gave birth to their son. He's now in an orphanage in
the countryside, and comes to see her from time to
time. Her prize possession is a photo of her and her
husband – both young fighters, idealistic and optimistic.

> Kabul, Afghanistan, March 11th 1996

Visit Pashtana, a widow, sewing in a freezing empty
room to earn a little to support the eight mouths
dependent on her. It's eight years since her husband
died. She has sold everything but the bare necessities.

Shamsergunj, Nepal, November 18th 2002

At a meeting with ActionAid partners discuss how the conflict here has affected local communities – not easy to travel around with frequent road-blocks, can't hold big meetings, never know when there will be a strike, some farmers have had a part of their harvest seized by the Maoists, who also demand donations from teachers and civil servants. Many village administration buildings have been destroyed so no citizenship papers are being issued – vital to do anything official, even open a bank account. Lots of early marriage, so young men are not seen as available for recruitment, by either side. We travel to a beautiful village set in the midst of paddy fields bathed in late afternoon light.

In a courtyard, women are winnowing their meagre rice harvest as they recount how their husbands and sons have disappeared. They have the traumatised look of those who do not understand why their lives have been turned upside down. Why the knocks on the door in the middle of the night, security forces taking men away, nothing heard since? Sixty-year-old Quisi is the most visibly upset – she has no children to help her, only two orphaned nephews to assist with the harvest ... she desperately misses her husband and is fearful of what has happened to him.

Kadhua, Rwanda, March 18th 1995

With Vicenze to the burial of a mass of people killed here during the genocide – an estimated total of 15,000 were slaughtered in the primary school and church. And twice as many in the rest of the commune. Vicenze's family were amongst them. Walk up to the church where there is a pyramid of skulls and sheeting with piles of half decomposed bodies. The February rains washed off the topsoil from where they had been buried, so those who did the killing were brought in to dig them up. Then the International Tribunal wanted to see the bodies, so the villagers have been waiting for a month for this service. The crossed fingers of one of the bodies seems like the saddest of gestures, not enough to prevent the killing of 99.5 % of the Tutsi population. Now Rwanda is a country of widows.

> Rombek, South Sudan, August 24th 1997

An endless drive to Rombek along sandy paths through vibrant green grass. Weird to be in a town, albeit one that is completely destroyed. Lots of foxholes and trenches where the Sudanese Government troops were living. Tour the damaged town, deserted apart from soldiers and a handful of old people who were left behind when everyone fled. Adeng Wul is completely despairing, hungry, abandoned and a scorpion bite on her hand is the latest of her woes. She dissolves in tears.

< Derry, Northern Ireland, February 2nd 1997

Relatives commemorate the 25th anniversary of
Bloody Sunday, when British soldiers opened fire on
a Civil Rights demonstration, killing 14.

Farida Afterwards

When I visited Afghanistan in December 2001, Farida Samadi was my translator, fixer and entertainer. Her English was a bit rusty after five years of enforced silence, but she took her job very seriously and delighted in showing me Kabul and introducing me to her women friends. It was an uncertain time. Like most women she still wore her burqa in public, but it was a pleasure to see her blossoming with the possibility of being herself and using the English that she had painstakingly studied.

'I'm the oldest in my family. I'm 28. I have two sisters and two brothers and I'm responsible for them. My father is a cook, my mother died two years ago – I miss her a lot, she was like my sister because she was only a bit older than me – just 40 – she was married at 12. I studied English at the University of Kabul, and then worked in the Ministry of Education writing books for elementary schools. I was the head of department. When the Taliban came we women lost our jobs straight away.

The ministry paid us for the first six months. For two years I did nothing then I got some odd bits of work. At the moment I'm doing cleaning work and preparing tea in a hospital. It's all very boring. Sometimes I cry because I'm educated and I could be doing something useful. It's very difficult that a woman with a bright brain has been kept away from society. Last week I registered as a teacher and I'm waiting to see if I can get my old job back.

The bombing of Kabul was very difficult for us – some of the bombs were in the wrong places and people were killed. But the Taliban time was terrible – men were beaten for not having beards, some so badly that they died. Women were picked up in the bazaar and taken to prison and beaten, and also raped there. We were terrified of them. They came to my house this time last year, just six days before the end of Ramadan. There were about 20 Talibs with guns, they came on a Saturday at midday and they burst into the house. They broke into the cupboard and took gold and the TV, video and cassettes. They took the things we enjoyed. When they were running things here I couldn't have my photo taken, I couldn't wear my Titanics (shoes with heels – although the film 'Titanic' was banned by the Taliban everyone seemed familiar with the costumes and hairstyles), we couldn't sing or dance. Even caged birds were not allowed – my heart was broken during that time.'

Kabul, Afghanistan, December 8th 2001

< Hanoi, Vietnam, August 20th 1991

Wars end. Great to cycle around a city I first knew as a news item on TV. Photograph lotus wreaths, monster creations of pink, bright yellow and green with a heady overwhelming smell. Have another puncture so spend 30 minutes sitting by the side of the road whilst one of the numerous repair-men fixes it – a ceremony involving meths and burning patches. Women gather round to look, a road worker buys me a banana and some children perform with hula hoops.

East London, South Africa, February 19th 1992

In a rundown primary school a dispirited headmaster catalogues the problems of his area – widespread TB, HIV, malnutrition, children molested in the communal toilets ending up with gonorrhoea ... gangs in the city who have proclaimed their aim is to rape all young women and make them pregnant. There's a crisis in education but at the same time this is part of a bigger structural crisis ... a breakdown in the fabric of society and a growth of violence that has moved from the political to the domestic arena. Repairing the damage of apartheid seems to be a much greater challenge than fighting against it was.

> Monrovia, Liberia, July 19th 1997

Sunny day and voters start queuing early. In spite of cynicism of crowds at the election rallies – at Charles Taylor's people chanted 'He kill my ma, He kill my pa, He'll get my vote' – today everyone seems to be taking it seriously. General Malu, the Nigerian in charge of ECOMOG, tours around checking everyone is being fair – the ECOMOG soldiers take pains to help those who can't understand the complicated voting form, although the sight of a large soldier with a big gun standing over a confused voter could be open to misunderstanding. After so many years of violence and terror, it's heartening to see people still believe elections can change things – the general feeling is that the best option is for Charles Taylor to be President – he would be much more dangerous in opposition.

Near Adequala, Eritrea, May 7th 1993

In the distance see a mass of people ambling along with picks and shovels – persuade Kelata to drive over the barren fields to them – turns out the whole community is building stone bunds to stop soil erosion, so when it rains the water will be retained ... the years of war and foraging for firewood have left a devastated landscape. This is a food for work scheme so everyone is moderately motivated, although it's the women who wield the pickaxes with most force, even when they are not being photographed. Most of them are working with babies strapped on their backs in cowry shell decorated papooses. Driving back to Asmara we give numerous people rides, one wonderful group of wild women ululate and dance when they are dropped off – magical.

> Usulutan, El Salvador, November 13th 1992

After years of road-blocks and complicated arrangements to reach areas controlled by the guerrillas (the FMLN), it's weird to be able to drive everywhere, and see such basic things as ex refugees busy building houses and reclaiming their communities. Milagros, an appropriate technology promoter, takes me to see the latrine building programme, which she runs with two other women. It takes them two days to make a toilet, a basic construction which makes life a thousand times more comfortable and healthy.

Grozny, Chechnya, June 7th 2000

To the railway station – the only hive of activity – in the midst of desolation, the surreal scene of 326 women rebuilding a station which has no trains. They have already replaced the white facade and slowly the mosaic floor is re-emerging. They are mostly widows, some of whose husbands have been taken to filtration camps. Ask why they are doing it. They reply, so that the city will exist again.

> Alkhan-Yurt, Chechnya, June 7th 2000

'Terrorism is a sickness. We from the Don are the cure', said the sign at the border-crossing checkpoint. In the first village we come to, 46 people were killed three months ago, and a several houses destroyed. It doesn't seem the Russians have the remedy but people are patching up their homes, joking with black humour, and quite expecting to be bombed again.

>> Kabul, Afghanistan, December 7th 2001

Mr K, the warm, kind-hearted worker at Care in charge of the Widows Programme, has offered to spend his day off with me. We (the entourage – Ali the driver, Farida, the giggly translator who keeps odd snacks in her handbag, determined that I shouldn't have to fast just because it's Ramadan, and I) set off for one of the Microrayons, the crumbling Soviet built blocks I had seen women making in 1988.

A gaggle of women totter towards us. Women might still be wearing burqas but they've gone overboard on inappropriate shoes – pointed toes and high heels reign in spite of the puddles and impossibility of really seeing where you are going when wearing a mesh in front of your eyes.

>> Kabul, Afghanistan, December 9th 2001

The radio has announced that teachers can register for the new term. At one of the registration centres, burqas cautiously greet burqas – then they are lifted to reveal the beaming faces of teachers who have been idle for five years whilst the Taliban forbade women to work and girls to study. There's a cautious optimism as to how long peace will last but everyone is thrilled to have the possibility of going to work.

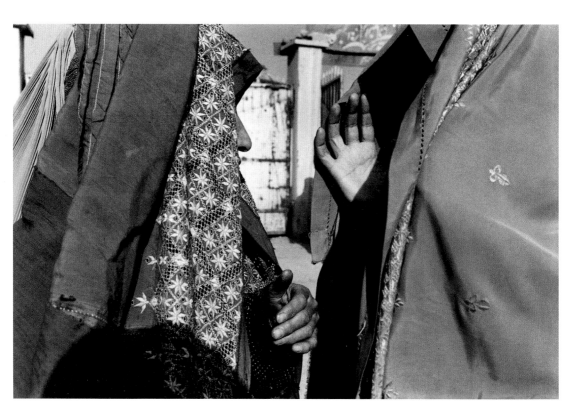

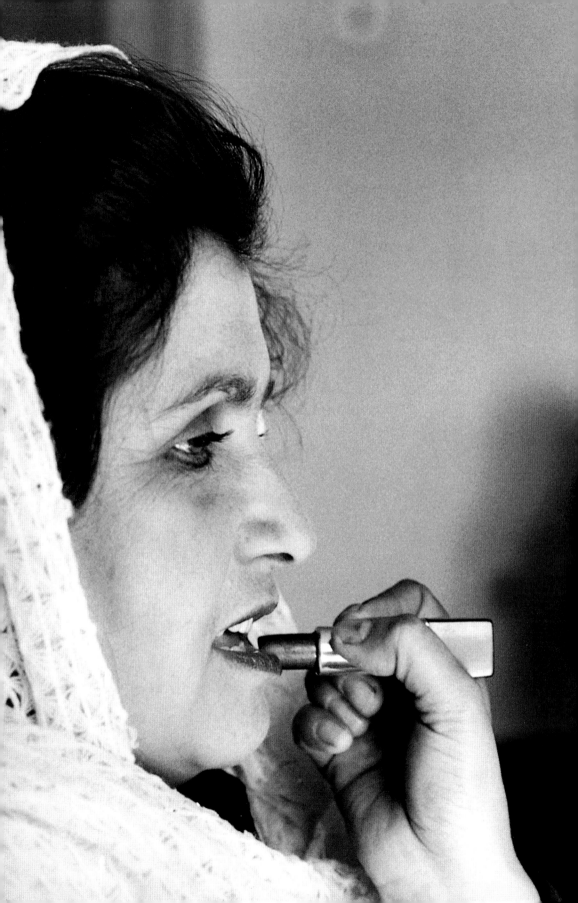

<<< Kabul, Afghanistan, December 8th 2001

At the university students have begun to register.
No one is sure when classes will start, or how.
The classrooms have nothing, often not even
windows, but there's an infectious mood of optimism.

<< Kabul, Afghanistan, December 7th 2001

I'd asked Mr K if he knows Razia, the female chowkidar
I'd met five years ago [see p 161]. Not only does he
know her but has got her address ... a knock on the
door, and she's there ... it's overwhelming to embrace
someone I've thought about a lot, whose photo has
been in exhibitions all over Europe, epitomising the
plight of Afghan widows. The warmth of friendship
surpasses the lack of a common language, it's so
wonderful to see her and her children. She still hangs
on to her photos of her disappeared husband, still
hoping he'll walk through the door. Jokingly I ask if
she's going to wear make-up now that the Taliban
have gone. She giggles, says it's been ten years since
she put on lipstick, but puts her hand into a bag and
pulls out a collection of beauty products. Farida leaps
into action and transforms Razia.

< Near Batticoloa, Sri Lanka, January 1st 2003

Drive through Tamil territory, past Tigers waiting for
peace to be formalised. At a memorial to fallen fighters
nine-month-old Thilipa and her mother wait for a bus –
normal life has resumed.

Women and War: country A-Z

Afghanistan

In 1979, the Soviet Union invaded Afghanistan to support the pro-communist regime, and spent the next ten years fighting US-backed mujahadeen rebels. The country descended into factional fighting after Soviet withdrawal in 1989. The Islamic fundamentalist Taliban took power in 1996, creating some stability, but imposing harsh strictures on Afghans, especially women. Following terrorist attacks on New York and Washington DC in September 2001, and the Taliban's refusal to hand over Osama Bin Laden, the US and its allies began military operations in the country, paving the way for the overthrow of the Taliban. Since December 2001, a UN-appointed interim government has brought some stability, but continued US military operations, ethnic unrest, banditry and an assassination attempt on the President in 2002 indicate a country still in turmoil.

Angola

War has blighted Angola for 27 years since independence from Portugal in 1975. At least half a million people have been killed, and four million displaced from their homes. The struggle is not just for power, but also for Angola's wealth of oil and diamonds. In 2002, the death of Jonas Savimbi, the leader of the UNITA rebels, led to a cease-fire and the first real hope of peace.

Bosnia Herzegovina

Yugoslavia fragmented in the early 1990s. Slobodan Milosevic, the leader of Yugoslavia's biggest state, Serbia, adopted fiercely nationalist policies. Fearing Serb domination and seeking their own independence, two of the six republics, Slovenia and Croatia, declared independence in 1991, followed in 1992 by Bosnia. In the resulting wars, some 200,000 people died, three million became refugees, and thousands of women were raped. The term 'ethnic cleansing' came into use, describing the systematic expulsion of one or more ethnic groups from villages where ethnic Serb, Croat and Muslim Bosnians had previously lived together.

Burma (Myanmar)

In multiparty elections in 1990, the Burmese people voted decisively for the main opposition party – led by charismatic leader Aung San Suu Kyi, daughter of the country's founding father General Aung San – but Burma's military rulers refused to relinquish power. She was placed under house arrest until 1995, ushering in a period of severe repression both of her followers and minority ethnic groups. An estimated 300,000 Shan, one of Burma's largest ethnic groups, have been displaced by the Burmese military, many hiding in the jungle with no food or medicine. In May 2002 Aung San Suu Kyi was released from a second period of house arrest, leading to some optimism that the military might eventually cede power.

Chechnya

Since 1991, rebels have fought to free Chechnya from Russian rule. The result has been devastation and terror. In 1994 Russian troops launched a brutal operation to quash the independence movement, and 100,000 people were killed over the next two years. Following Russian withdrawal in 1996, Chechnya enjoyed some autonomy, but it remained a lawless place where violence and kidnappings were common. After several bomb attacks in 1999, the Russians launched a second military campaign to restore control. Appalling human rights abuses have been committed by both sides,

thousands of refugees have fled to neighbouring states and the capital Grozny has been virtually levelled.

Colombia

A three-cornered fight between government forces, left-wing guerrillas and right-wing paramilitaries has devastated Colombia since the 1980s, with over 4,000 non-combatants now killed each year. Almost three million people have been forcibly displaced. The involvement of drug traffickers has further complicated the situation: drug-related crime is now the second largest cause of death, and has given Colombia the world's highest kidnap rate. Colombia's internal war intensified in 2002 following the collapse of peace talks between the government and the largest guerrilla group, FARC.

Croatia

Croatia and Slovenia, two of the six Yugoslav republics, declared independence from Belgrade in 1991. Slovenia was allowed to leave Yugoslavia after a 10-day war, but Croatia's bid was opposed by its ethnic Serb minority and the Serb government in Belgrade. In the war that followed, around 10,000 people died, several Croatian towns were destroyed and, in 1995, tens of thousands of Serbs were forced out of Croatia and into Serbia. Several Croatian military leaders are on trial at the International Criminal Tribunal for the Former Yugoslavia in The Hague.

El Salvador

The US administration armed right-wing government forces against left-wing guerrillas during El Salvador's 12-year civil war, which began in 1980 and left 70,000 people dead. Shadowy right-wing death squads killed thousands of people, including Archbishop Oscar Romero of San Salvador. The 1992 peace treaty brought the war to an end and precipitated important political reforms. Although they have been identified, many of those responsible for massacres, extra-judicial executions, disappearances and assassinations have yet to be tried or punished. Since the end of the war, El Salvador has been hit by a series of natural disasters, notably Hurricane Mitch in 1998, and a number of earthquakes in 2001.

Eritrea

For 30 years Eritrea struggled for independence from Ethiopia, which annexed it in 1962. In 1991 the Marxist regime fell in Addis Ababa, the Eritrean People's Liberation Front defeated government forces, and a provisional government was established. Two years later Eritreans voted overwhelmingly for independence in a UN-monitored referendum. A border war with Ethiopia erupted in 1998. Very little land changed hands, over 70,000 people were killed and, despite a peace treaty in 2000, Eritrea has been reduced to penury as its people face the gigantic task of rebuilding their country.

Ethiopia

In 1974, after a devastating famine, Ethiopia's Emperor Haile Selassie was overthrown. The military junta which followed, known as the Derg, was made up of ruthless Marxists who brought nearly two decades of war, repression and, again, periodic famine. The Derg was finally toppled by a coalition of rebel forces in 1991, creating a degree of political and economic stability. The benefits of peace, however, were squandered in 1998 during a two-year border war with neighbouring Eritrea in which over 70,000 people were killed. Ethiopia remains one of Africa's poorest countries, and in 2002 faced famine once again.

Guatemala

Civil war began in Guatemala in 1960. Along with El Salvador and Nicaragua, the country also suffered from the Cold War politics of the late 20th century. The USA had a hand in toppling several governments and, in the 1980s, right-wing death squads killed thousands of peasants. In 1996, the government signed a peace agreement formally ending the 36-year conflict, which had led to the death and disappearance of over 200,000 people and had created a million refugees. Although an official report found that 93% of atrocities were carried out by the security forces, the corrupt justice system and a still-powerful military have ensured delays in bringing those responsible to account.

Haiti

A violent coup in Haiti in 1991 overthrew the government of Jean Bertrand Aristide, the first democratically elected president after more than three decades of dictatorship and provisional governments. Several thousand Haitians were killed in the three years of de facto military rule that followed. Economic hardship and worsening human rights abuses forced thousands of Haitians to seek refuge in neighbouring countries, including the US. Although civilian rule was restored in 1994, elections have since been plagued by allegations of fraud and irregularities. The return of Aristide to power in 2000 after a controversial election has not led to stability and Haiti remains the poorest country in the western hemisphere.

Honduras

Although Honduras has not been at war since the infamous Football War with El Salvador in 1969, the country was affected by events in neighbouring countries throughout the 1980s. US-backed Contra rebels, waging a guerrilla war against the Sandinista regime in Nicaragua, used Honduras as a training and staging ground. The US also built bases to train Honduran and Salvadoran troops to fight leftist guerrillas, while thousands of refugees from El Salvador and Guatemala were held virtual prisoners in refugee camps. After a decade of peace, Honduras was devastated by Hurricane Mitch in 1998, which left more than 5,000 people dead and 1.5 million displaced.

Iraq

Saddam Hussein came to power in 1979 and invaded neighbouring Iran the following year. Since then Iraqis have known nothing but war and deprivation. The conflict with Iran lasted eight years. Iraq subsequently invaded Kuwait in 1991, but was driven out by a US-led coalition. International sanctions have had a devastating effect on the country's economy and society, leading to the death of a million children, according to UN figures. After the Gulf War, the UN required Iraq to surrender all chemical and biological weapons and long-range missiles, and to allow in UN weapons inspectors. The inspectors were withdrawn in 1998, but were allowed to return in 2002 under threat of a new US-led war.

Kosovo

The conflict in Kosovo marked the last stand of Slobodan Milosevic, former president of Serbia who was now president of what remained of Yugoslavia – the federation of Serbia and Montenegro. His suppression of the majority Albanian population in Serbia's formerly autonomous Kosovo province led to civil war. Albanian guerrillas committed some atrocities but Serb forces carried out widespread 'ethnic cleansing', executions and other human rights abuses. NATO forces went to the aid of the Albanian population in 1999, with an intensive bombing campaign of Serbia and Kosovo. Milosevic was overthrown in 2000 and, in 2002, brought before the International Criminal Tribunal for the Former Yugoslavia in The Hague.

Liberia

Liberia was created in 1847 as a haven for freed slaves from America. It has since become one of the most violent countries in Africa. Civil war started in 1989 when rebel leader, Charles Taylor, began an uprising and over the following years took control of most of the country but not the capital, Monrovia. The conflict, which also affected neighbouring countries including Sierra Leone and Guinea, lasted until 1997 and during this time at least 150,000 people were killed. Charles Taylor, who became president following elections in 1997, is widely regarded as a cruel and capricious leader profiting from the illegal trade in diamonds and logging. Rival factions still vie for power.

Mozambique

A civil war followed shortly after Mozambique's independence from Portugal in 1975, and did not end until 1992. The right-wing guerrillas trying to overthrow the Marxist government were backed first by Rhodesia (now Zimbabwe), then South Africa. The war led to famine in the mid 1980s, caused the deaths of at least 100,000 people and the creation of more than a million refugees. Under the peace treaty that ended the war, the rebel movement transformed itself into a political party challenging the ruling party peacefully and Mozambique is seen by some as a promising democracy and a model for reconciliation. Devastating floods in 2000 brought more hardship, with a million people forced to flee their homes.

Nepal

Nepal is the world's only Hindu kingdom. In 1990 King Birendra ceded absolute power but this did not bring political stability. A Maoist movement launched a 'people's war' in 1996 fighting to overthrow a government they accuse of having failed to develop Nepal's rural areas. The conflict has claimed 7,000 lives over the past seven years – 5,000 have died at the hands of government forces with a further 2,000 killed by the Maoists. Further economic and political strain is placed on Nepal by the 2,500 Tibetan refugees fleeing through the country every year to India – home of the exiled Tibetan government. In June 2001, Crown Prince Dipendra killed nine members of his family, including the King, before turning the gun on himself.

Nicaragua

After overthrowing Nicaragua's right-wing Somoza dictatorship in 1979, the Sandinistas – named after nationalist hero Augusto Sandino – tried to bring in land reform and social change. But the Reagan administration armed right-wing guerrillas – the Contras – and a vicious civil war ensued, overshadowing positive reforms in literacy, education and healthcare. The US continued to fund the Contras throughout the 1980s, by the end of which the Sandinistas had lost popularity due to economic mismanagement and corruption. A series of centre-right governments have been elected since 1990. The country slowly rebuilt its economy, but was hit hard by Hurricane Mitch in 1998, which left 10,000 people dead.

Northern Ireland

In 1800 Ireland was incorporated into the United Kingdom, a move that angered the catholic-dominated south. By 1920 a campaign of guerrilla warfare by the IRA had forced the British government to grant independence to the south, leaving the mainly protestant north as part of the UK. The recent conflict began in 1969, when Britain took control of Northern Ireland's security forces. A number of paramilitary organisations sprang up and, between 1969 and 1994, more than 3,000 people died in the violent conflict, known as 'the Troubles', that followed. In April 1998, following tough negotiations, the Good Friday Peace Agreement was signed. Relative peace has since reigned, although the path remains uncertain.

Palestine

The creation of the Jewish state of Israel in 1948 forced 780,000 Palestinians into exile in neighbouring countries. In 1967, after attacks from Arab states, Israeli forces occupied the Palestinian areas of the Gaza Strip and the West Bank, and started settling there. In 1993, after decades of violent conflict between Israelis and Palestinians, leaders of both sides agreed to the signing of a historic peace accord, which was supposed to grant more autonomy to Palestinians in the Gaza Strip and the West Bank. However, tensions continued between the two states and in 2000 violence flared up again. A peace process still has not been agreed.

Rwanda

In one of the worst mass crimes of the 20th century, some 800,000 Rwandans were killed in a few months in 1994. Most were ethnic Tutsis, Rwanda's minority group. Rivalry between the Tutsis and the majority Hutus festered after the country's independence from Belgium in 1959, and reached a peak in the early 1990s when a group of armed Tutsis launched a civil war from their base in Uganda. After the 1994 genocide the main Hutu leaders were arrested and taken to the International Criminal Tribunal for Rwanda. Vast numbers of ordinary Hutus fled to Zaire (now Democratic Republic of Congo), where vengeance and war continued.

Sierra Leone

Sierra Leone has become a byword for cruelty – the rebels who launched a civil war in the 1990s raped and mutilated thousands, often cutting off the limbs of innocent civilians to intimidate the government. A Nigerian-led west African peacekeeping force also killed and maimed, while all factions scrambled for control of the country's diamond mines. After intervention by the UN in 1999 warring factions signed a peace agreement and British and UN peacekeeping forces were able to disarm the rebels. A war crimes tribunal has been established, and peaceful elections were held in May 2002.

South Africa

Racial segregation and inequality had existed as a matter of custom and practice for decades in South Africa, but in 1948 were enacted in law. Since its founding in 1912, the African National Congress (ANC) had led non-violent protests against segregation and, in 1952, launched the Defiance Campaign against the apartheid laws. In 1960, following the Sharpeville massacre and the banning of the ANC, supporters began to form militant groups in order to launch an armed struggle. In the early 1960s, leaders of the ANC, including Nelson Mandela, and other anti-apartheid activists were arrested and sentenced to life imprisonment. It was to take another 30 years of violence and racial intolerance before Mandela was released in 1990. South African's first non-racial democratic election was held in 1994, with Mandela winning the presidency. A Truth and Reconciliation Commission was established in 1996 as a way of healing the country's deep racial and political rifts.

Sri Lanka

Conflict between the Sinhalese majority and the Tamil minority has persisted throughout most of Sri Lanka's history. An all-out civil war broke out in the early 1980s and, to date, an estimated 64,000 people have been killed. In 2002 a successful peace initiative by the Norwegian government resulted in a ceasefire, which many hope will bring an end to nearly two decades of violence.

Sudan

In nearly five decades of independence, Sudan has only experienced one decade of peace. More than two million people, mainly from the south, have died while five million people – 80% of the population – have been displaced in the last 20 years. Famine, caused by war, has killed more than fighting. Government is dominated by Muslim Arabs from the north, but most southerners are Africans, either Christian or following traditional religions, and this divide is a major cause of war. At the end of 2002, a new peace initiative and the promise of economic development from oil exploration gave some hope of peace.

Uganda

Hundreds of thousands of Ugandans perished under Idi Amin, who governed from 1971-79, and Milton Obote in the early 1980s. Yoweri Museveni's revolutionary forces marched into Kampala in 1986 and established peace in the centre and west of the country. The north, however, has not enjoyed the benefits of Uganda's economic boom. A sect called the Lord's Resistance Army seizes children and takes them to southern Sudan while, in the northeast, the Karamojong habitually raid neighbouring districts and have forced over 80,000 people into displacement camps.

United Kingdom

Britain used to have an empire that, at its height, covered a quarter of the world's land area, giving it historical links with a variety of countries, and more influence than its size merits. The only unilateral war the UK has fought in recent times was with Argentina over the Falkland Islands. British troops fought as part of a US-led coalition in the Gulf to oust Iraq from Kuwait and have also been involved in numerous UN missions. In 2001, over 70,000 people migrated to the UK seeking asylum. Under Prime Minister Tony Blair, Britain has tried to add an 'ethical dimension' to its foreign policy, but many see its status as the world's second largest arms supplier as belying such ambitions.

United States of America

After the collapse of the Soviet Union in 1991, the USA became the world's sole superpower. It has the largest economy in the world with a defence budget of US$396 billion. During the Cold War, the US funded rebel groups and governments which it believed were fighting communism. Following the attacks on New York and Washington DC on 11 September 2001, it launched a 'war on terror'. This began with the war against the Taliban in Afghanistan. President George Bush later labelled North Korea, Iraq and Iran as the 'axis of evil' – countries which he said were developing chemical and biological weapons and might therefore pose a threat to the USA. In March 2003, a US-led coalition attacked Iraq.

Vietnam

Vietnam gained independence from France in 1954, but remained divided and unstable for many years afterwards. The country's bloodiest war was fought between communist North Vietnam and US-backed South Vietnam, a war that claimed around two million lives. The use of Agent Orange and other defoliants left ten million hectares of productive land barren, and many thousands of civilians suffering from disease and abnormalities. The Vietnam War officially ended in 1973, but Vietnam continued to be involved in conflict, most notably with Cambodia and China.

Zaire (now Democratic Republic of Congo)

Zaire was born in blood. The first president, Patrice Lumumba, was deposed then assassinated only months after coming to power at independence in 1960. His successor, Mobutu Sese Seko, ruled by fear for more than 30 years. Reportedly stealing billions of dollars from export earnings and Western aid, he became fabulously wealthy while his people grew poor and desperate. The arrival of a million refugees from Rwanda in 1994 brought war and further suffering. Laurent Kabila ousted Mobutu in 1997 but his regime was soon challenged by a Rwanda-backed rebellion.

Other neighbouring countries also became embroiled in the conflict which has led to an estimated two million deaths. Kabila was assassinated in 2001 and was succeeded by his son, Joseph, who signed a peace accord with the warring factions in July 2002.

> Freetown, Sierra Leone, May 8th 2002

Saffie (centre) is blind. Her eyes cut out by rebels and given to her father.